PERSPECTIVES ON COGNITIVE PSYCHOLOGY

COGNITIVE BEHAVIORAL THERAPY

NEW RESEARCH

PERSPECTIVES ON COGNITIVE PSYCHOLOGY

Additional books in this series can be found on Nova's website under the Series tab.

Additional e-books in this series can be found on Nova's website under the e-book tab.

PERSPECTIVES ON COGNITIVE PSYCHOLOGY

COGNITIVE BEHAVIORAL THERAPY

NEW RESEARCH

BRENDAN MYERS
EDITOR

NOVINKA
New York

For permission to use material from this book please contact us:
Telephone 631-231-7269; Fax 631-231-8175
Web Site: http://www.novapublishers.com

LIBRARY OF CONGRESS CATALOGING-IN-PUBLICATION DATA

Cognitive behavioral therapy : new research / editor, Brendan Myers.
pages cm. -- (Perspectives on cognitive psychology)
Includes index.
ISBN: 978-1-63321-638-9 (softcover)
1. Cognitive therapy. I. Myers, Brendan.
RC489.C63C6417 2014
616.89'1425--dc23

2014028261

Published by Nova Science Publishers, Inc. † New York

CONTENTS

PREFACE

This book begins by briefly reviewing the challenges that clinicians face, working with children in the new health care era. The book then discusses trauma focused CBT for children with developmental disabilities; CBT for informal cancer caregivers; CBT in pain management of adult chronic nonmalignant pain patients; and CBT for rheumatoid arthritis.

Chapter 1 – The Affordable Care Act (ACA) has altered the landscape of health care by forcing behavioral health workers from their silos into a rapidly changing, fast-paced, integrative care setting of increased accountability and accessibility. In order to survive in this transition, behavioral health care will have to be transportable beyond traditional one-to-one psychotherapy models, be viewed as a less consumable commodity, and be able to efficiently treat the myriad of comorbid psychological disorders that present in every area of medicine. Fortunately, cognitive behavioral therapy (CBT) enjoys a long tradition of empirical success with a wide variety of clinical disorders in youth. Accordingly, CBT provides a robust platform from which to launch new clinical models and delivery systems beyond the limitations of a single-disorder paradigm to target transdiagnostic factors that perpetuate psychological disorders in youth. This chapter briefly reviews the challenges that face clinicians working with children in the new health care era. Second, the emergence transdiagnostic modular CBT will be described and this approach aligns with initiatives put forth by the National Institute of Mental Health as well as the ACA will be presented. Thirdly, the issues surrounding disseminating competent training models of transdiagnostic modular CBT will addressed. Finally, recommendations for increasing accountability, branding services, and increasing consumers' mental health literacy to obviate commoditization will be provided. Transdiagnostic modular CBT is the future of behavioral health care and the future is NOW!

Chapter 2 – Trauma-Focused Cognitive Behavioral Therapy (TF-BT) has strong empirical evidence of its effectiveness to treat Post-Traumatic Stress Disorder (PTSD) in children. Recently, some state licensing and oversight authorities have mandated that mental health providers use this protocol for children. Such mandates are often made without regard to diagnosis or intellectual functioning that might predict TF-CBT efficacy. However, no research has been conducted regarding the use of TF-CBT among the intellectually disabled population. Therefore, this study sought to fill this gap in the literature and determine if manualized TF-CBT was as effective as more traditional behaviorally based approaches. Results demonstrate that manualized TF-BT was less effective than behaviorally based approaches for children with cognitive disabilities. Implications of this research are discussed.

Chapter 3 – The experience of providing care to a loved one with cancer is associated with significant psychological, physical, temporal, and financial burden. A growing number of interventions have been developed to address the psychological component of burden among informal cancer caregivers (ICs), of which cognitive behavioral therapies (CBTs) have shown particularly promising results. No overall synthesis of CBTs for ICs exists, and the present chapter therefore provides a systematic review of previous studies of CBTs for ICs, their target outcomes, therapeutic components, and effects. The authors conclude that although their knowledge of the burden experienced by caregivers has increased over the past decade, this knowledge has not yet been sufficiently translated into effective interventions for caregivers. Informed by recent advances in the affective sciences, this chapter presents emotion regulation as an important target for future interventions. The authors argue that the distress experienced by ICs can be conceptualized as products of maladaptive regulation of the motivational and emotional conflicts associated with providing care. Based on this model, recommendations for future CBT interventions are provided.

Chapter 4 – The origin, course and subsequent maintenance of pain is influenced by psychosocial factors. For this reason, psychotherapy is also used in pain management and the use of cognitive behavioral therapy (CBT) is dominant. This chapter describes the history of CBT and its three basic approaches: behavioral, cognitive and cognitive-behavioral. The indication to CBT and the most frequent problems in treatment are defined. Basic CBT techniques in chronic pain management, namely cognitive restructuring and the practice of skills for pain and stress management (education, adaptive positive self-instruction, relaxation and imagination, graded activity, exposition, structured problem solving and relapse coping) are specified. Particular fields of chronic pain which represent the goal of the multidisciplinary program of pain management including CBT are examined. The authors structure the basic assumptions of a successful program: direct and indirect positive reinforcement of pain behavior, positive reinforcement of required behavior, improvement of physical condition, cognitive reframing, education, training in CBT in pain management and conforming to CBT principles. The chapter summarizes the efficiency of CBT in chronic non-malignant pain management in adult patients, describes problems in its monitoring and suggests some innovations increasing its use.

Chapter 5 – Rheumatoid arthritis (RA) is an autoimmune, chronic, degenerative, progressive and disabling disease that affects about 1% of world population. RA patients suffer from persistent pain with acute attacks during crises. In addition, they also present stiffness, swelling, and loss of mobility due to inflammation of the joints. There are also less common symptoms such as fever, weakness, loss of appetite and sleepiness alteration. The most commonly damaged joints are knees, feet, hands, wrists, elbows, neck and the temporomandibular region, which are affected during the disease progression causing severe deformities, osteoarthritis, tendon rupture and decrease of the life expectancy of the patient in five to ten years. Besides, psychiatric comorbidities such as anxiety, depression and risk of suicide and para-suicide, have high prevalence in RA affecting the prognosis of RA and worsening the overall picture and the intensity of pain as well as compromising the ability of adherence to treatment. Cognitive-Behavioral Therapy for RA patients seeks not only the reduction of psychiatric comorbidities, such as anxiety and depression, for which this therapeutic model has already proved effective, but also for resolving specific issues of the clinical course of RA. Dysfunctional thoughts related to physical changes, deformities and body image perception are evaluated and restructured when necessary, as well as problem solving techniques are applied to identify new forms of everyday functioning, facilitating de rehabilitation of the patient considering the existence of physical limitations. Psychoeducation is useful to equip the patient to meet the challenges arising from the progress of the disease, and also the medical treatment. Pain control techniques are used to help patients to recognize and management the stimulus and situations that can worsening or reduce pain. New behaviors are developed to enable the performance of daily activities, considering the limitations imposed by the disease. With new coping behaviors, the patient starts to develop new thoughts about the disease, of him and of the future. Thus, it becomes possible to have a higher quality of life. Here the authors present a literature review on the topic, as well as a proposal for cognitive-behavioral treatment for RA considering its clinical challenges and, finally, are presented a case report.

In: Cognitive Behavioral Therapy
Editor: Brendan Myers

ISBN: 978-1-63321-638-9

Chapter 1

The Future Is NOW!: Transdiagnostic Modular CBT and Health Care Reform

Paul J. Sullivan, Marisa Keller, Micaela Thordarson, Sandra Trafalis and Robert D. Friedberg
Center for the Study and Treatment of Anxious Youth
at Palo Alto University, CA, US

Abstract

The Affordable Care Act (ACA) has altered the landscape of health care by forcing behavioral health workers from their silos into a rapidly changing, fast-paced, integrative care setting of increased accountability and accessibility. In order to survive in this transition, behavioral health care will have to be transportable beyond traditional one-to-one psychotherapy models, be viewed as a less consumable commodity, and be able to efficiently treat the myriad of comorbid psychological disorders that present in every area of medicine. Fortunately, cognitive behavioral therapy (CBT) enjoys a long tradition of empirical success with a wide variety of clinical disorders in youth. Accordingly, CBT provides a robust platform from which to launch new clinical models and delivery systems beyond the limitations of a single-disorder paradigm to target transdiagnostic factors that perpetuate psychological disorders in youth. This chapter briefly reviews the challenges that face clinicians working with children in the new health care era. Second, the emergence transdiagnostic modular CBT will be described and this approach aligns with initiatives put forth by the National Institute of Mental Health as well as the ACA will be presented. Thirdly, the issues surrounding disseminating competent training models of transdiagnostic modular CBT will addressed. Finally, recommendations for increasing accountability, branding services, and increasing consumers' mental health literacy to obviate commoditization will be provided. Transdiagnostic modular CBT is the future of behavioral health care and the future is NOW!

Keywords: Transdiagnostic, modular, CBT, health care, youth, children

INTRODUCTION

Weary ideas and tattered care models are out of place in the era of health care reform. Funding initiatives from the National Institute of Mental Health (NIMH) are drifting away from a reliance on specific diagnostic taxonomies such as the DSM-5 and the ICD-11 (Cuthbert & Insel, 2013). Both the NIMH and transdiagnostic modular cognitive behavior therapy (CBT) focus on common pathways contributing to multiple disorders. Fresh perspectives and mint-condition paradigms are required.

Transdiagnostic modular CBT represents such a progressive approach. Transdiagnostic CBT is well-matched to the Accountable and Affordable Care Act (ACA) as well as NIMH funding initiatives. A transdiagnostic approach eludes the conundrums associated with various iterations of the Diagnostic Statistical Manuals (DSM) and International Classification of Diseases (ICD). Finally, a modular format solves various dilemmas posed by multiple treatment manuals.

This chapter details the seismic shifts the ACA brings to the behavioral health care landscape. Accountable, integrated behavioral health care marked by quality indicators marks the new normal. Cognitive behavioral clinicians are likely to be co-located in schools as well as pediatricians' offices. The chapter also includes a section highlighting the compatibility of transdiagnostic modular CBT with ACA imperatives. Finally, the chapter concludes by emphasizing salient issues associated with proper dissemination and training.

A Brand New World!: Health Care Imperatives

The current state of mental health care for youth is disappointing. Most children in need do not receive the care they deserve (Nash, Cubic, Khatri, & Baird, 2013). Further, treatment as usual in community care settings yields an effect size of zero (Garland et al., 2013; Warren et al., 2010), indicating that even those who access services do not receive effective care. Not coincidentally, the rates of polypharmacy and prescription of atypical anti-psychotic medicines are skyrocketing (Comer & Barlow, 2014). As the health care system transforms under the imperatives guiding Patient Protection and Affordable Care Act (ACA), mental health services must prove their value.

The ACA initiated a major renovation of the health care system in the United States. Simply, the ACA aspires to improve access, quality of care, and concurrently contain costs (Kelly & Coons, 2012). Emphasis on evidence-based practices and use of outcome metrics will propel better clinical care. Changes in behavioral health care mandate patient protection and, accordingly, reforms draw significant focus to clinical accountability. Essentially, accountability means bringing good outcomes to patient care (Rozensky & Janicke, 2012). More specifically, the ACA emphasizes accountability for health care providers with incentive based pay-for-performance benefits (Asarnow & Miranda, 2014; Berwick, Nolan, & Whittington, 2008).

In the near future, mental health care will be increasingly integrated into primary care, with an emphasis on primary and secondary prevention (Nordal, 2012). The implementation of Patient Centered Medical Homes and emergence of School Based Health Centers instantiate this trend (Department of Health and Human Services, 2012c; Kelly & Coons, 2012). The ACA mandates insurance coverage of 13 behavioral health services for all children as well as the assessment screening for depression, obesity-related disorders, drug, and alcohol use in adolescents (Department of Health and Human Services, 2012b; Tynan & Woods, 2013). Due to this welcome revamping of the health care system, primary health care and behavioral health care are fused.

The new system aims to augment patient outcomes by transitioning to integrated primary care. Integrated care requires a total transformation of practice and perspective, not a simple face-lift of aging service lines (Vogel, 2012). New skills must be developed and mental health practitioners must be prepared to interact regularly and fluently with physicians. This requires becoming comfortable with medical terminology, ease with hallway hand-offs, and intervening skillfully in 15-20 minute sessions (Vogel, 2012). Historically, medical and mental health services are delivered in silos. However, seamless integration with interprofessional care teams is now the objective (Nordal, 2012). Instead of individual providers treating patients' emotional problems independently, health care professionals are charged with collaborating on a continua of clinical care.

While children and adolescents present with behavioral health issues in primary care settings, very few children actually receive treatment in this system that is ill-equipped to handle behavioral health issues (Ward-Zimmerman & Cannata, 2012). Behavioral health clinicians will increasingly need to partner with pediatricians and other primary care providers to support the early detection, intervention, and treatment of children and adolescents (Drotar, 2013). Medical services do not routinely include formal screenings or risk assessments. When these assessments are conducted, only a small proportion of children and youth actually enter treatment even when referred (Fine & Mayer, 2006). The paucity of treatment options in a primary care setting, the lack of appropriate linkages to services, and the inability for current medical systems to effectively intervene and treat behavioral disorders among youth mean that the potential for improved care is immense (Drotar, 2013; Ward-Zimmerman & Cannata, 2012).

Providers placed in internal medicine and OB/GYN departments will deliver care to parents in the form of augmentation of prenatal care, decreased parental substance abuse, increased family functioning, and better parenting skills (Tynan & Woods, 2013). Clinicians in family medicine, pediatrics, and specialized pediatric wards (e.g. pediatric oncology, organ transplants, etc.) will provide direct behavioral health care to young patients (Black, 2002; Tynan & Woods, 2013). For the first time, behavioral health care clinicians will be practicing in virtually every area of medicine.

With emphasis shifted towards prevention, ACA provides for 26 emotional and behavioral health screens across the development of children (Black, 2002). Physicians will rely on mental health care providers to complete these evaluations (Black, 2002; Tynan & Woods, 2013). Beidas et al. (2014) facilitated this screening process with a listing of low-cost, valid, and reliable measures for common problems. The ACA's funded School-Based Health Centers (SBHCs) serve as the "front lines" for providing comprehensive health care to youth who rarely access preventive mental health services (North, McElligot, Douglas, & Martin, 2014). SBHCs allow unprecedented accessibility to traditionally under-served individuals (Bains, Franzen, & White-Freseé, 2014).

Kolko and Perrin (2014) reviewed the current literature on the integration of behavioral health care in comprehensive pediatric care settings. They highlighted the applicability of transdiagnostic modular intervention in pediatric settings. Modular treatments target common elements of disorders, are time-efficient, and assist in pushing the field toward compatibility with primary health care clinics. Kolko and Perrin concluded that transdiagnostic modular interventions enjoy real-world applicability that reduces symptoms, improves functioning, and fits well within the fast-paced pediatric setting.

Sobel and colleagues (2001) implemented a multivariate outcomes measurement system in an existing integrated pediatric primary care setting where 89% of patients received CBT interventions. Objective measures reflected significant improvements in patient distress; 78% of parents reported their children fell within the absent to mild range of symptoms after receiving the intervention.

Weersing, Rozenman, Maher-Bridge, and Campo (2012) built a transdiagnostic toolbox for pediatric practice. They created two brief behavioral therapies that target co-occurring anxiety, depression, and somatic problems. Both treatment protocols implemented patient-specific modular approaches that use basic CBT interventions (psychoeducation, relaxation) while integrating exposure and behavioral activation. Weersing et al. found these interventions were not only effective, but facilitated dissemination to pediatric settings with cost effectiveness and flexibility.

Welcome Harmony: Modular CBT and the Health Care Imperatives

CBT-spectrum approaches enjoy a long-standing tradition of empirical support (Shafran et al., 2009). These favorable results spawned a proliferation of manualized treatments for specific disorders leading to a virtual alphabet soup for clinicians (e.g. CBT for Depression, CBT for GAD, CBT for OCD) (Friedberg & Breslford, 2011). Additionally, these discrete manuals focusing on single disorders differ from each other in non-significant ways (Kendall, Gosch, Furr, & Sood, 2008; Weisz & Chorpita, 2012, Wilamowska, Thompson-Hollands, Fairholme, Ellard, Farchione, & Barlow, 2010).

CBT is migrating toward transdiagnostic treatments that address multiple disorders, rather than remaining stuck in the conventional single-disorder paradigm. Transdiagnostic treatment approaches yield several advantages over disorder-specific interventions (Weersing, et al., 2012). First, they emphasize common factors that underlie multiple disorders, and are therefore capable of conceptualizing and treating comorbidity (Weersing et al., 2012). Youth rarely present with a single circumscribed disorder indicating comorbidity is the rule, rather than the exception (Weersing et al., 2012; Wilamowska et al., 2010). Comorbidity greatly complicates treatment decisions, as it can alter how to prioritize treatment when most evidence-based interventions are designed with a single disorder in mind (Weersing et al., 2012). Transdiagnostic approaches elegantly address this issue by targeting the shared underlying constructs that contribute to multiple disorders, rather than conceptualizing the disorders as discrete and unrelated entities.

There is a growing body of research demonstrating the efficacy of transdiagnostic treatment approaches in youth and adults. The Unified Protocol for Emotional Disorders (UP; Wilamowska et al., 2010) addresses a broad spectrum of internalizing symptoms, rather than focusing on a specific anxiety or depressive disorder. This approach acknowledges the particularly high rate of comorbidity that exists among internalizing disorders (Wilamowska et al., 2010), and preliminary findings suggest that this approach is promising with both adults and adolescents (Ehrenreich, Goldstein, Wright, & Barlow, 2009; Wilamowska et al., 2010).

One particular strategy for developing transdiagnostic treatments for youth is to distill the procedures common across evidence-based treatments into "modules" that can be selected and arranged according to each individual's needs and circumstances (Friedberg et al., 2011; Weisz & Chorpita, 2012). A modular approach to transdiagnostic CBT further extends the improvements upon the original single-disorder system by increasing clinicians' ability to tailor treatments to each patient. Modular treatments developed out of the finding that most evidence-based interventions shared many commonalities, including specific procedures that appear to be critical to the treatment of specific problems (Wilamowska et al., 2010). By distilling the many effective treatments down to their shared elements, "modules" are constructed that are composed of general procedures which can then be selected and arranged as needed for an individual (Weisz & Chorpita, 2012)

The literature suggests that greater individualization in treatment yields improved treatment outcomes (Chorpita et al., 2004). However, this increased flexibility must be balanced against the importance of maintaining fidelity to the treatment protocol (Kendall et al., 2008). Lack of structure can compromise the effectiveness of an intervention and lead to worse outcomes (Chorpita et al., 2004). Modular CBT seeks to balance these goals of providing structured, empirically-supported interventions that can be flexibly tailored to each child. Modular CBT explicitly incorporates clinician judgment and flexibility into the protocol, allowing clinicians to respond to crises as well as changes in symptomology, comorbidity, and treatment response while remaining faithful to the protocol (Weisz & Chorpita, 2012). Clinicians therefore become active participants in treatment planning and implementation, rather than passively following a prescribed session sequence.

Modular CBT typically includes psychoeducation, self-monitoring, behavioral interventions, cognitive restructuring, basic behavioral tasks, and experiments and exposures (Friedberg & Brelsford, 2011). Psychoeducation involves providing youth and their parents with information about the presenting problems and treatment approach, which facilitates motivation and treatment buy-in. Self-monitoring includes tracking a children's thoughts, feelings, and behaviors, in order to increase awareness and establish a baseline. Cognitive restructuring strategies are aimed at altering thought content and processes, and include: decatastrophizing, test of evidence, and reattribution. Basic behavioral tasks involve building skills such as problem solving, relaxation training, and social skills. Finally, experiments and exposures are a critical module that encourages performance attainment and mastery experiences where the child applies new skills in real world situations, thereby reducing experiential avoidance and increasing self-efficacy.

Weisz and Chorpita (2012) developed the Modular Approach to Therapy for Children with Anxiety, Depression, Trauma, or Conduct Problems (MATCH-ADTC), which is a comprehensive set of treatment procedures as well as decision-making flowcharts that guide treatment through each of the four listed problem areas. MATCH-ADTC is an exemplar of modular CBT in its use of "core" procedures for each problem area (e.g., psychoeducation, self-monitoring, and exposure are the core procedures for anxiety) as well as procedures used for "managing obstacles" that may arise during the course of treatment. Clinicians use the guiding flow charts to decide upon treatment focus, make decisions about which modules to use and in what order, and evaluate treatment progress.

Preliminary findings support the effectiveness of modular treatment approaches. For example, Weisz and colleagues (2012) compared modular CBT to both standard (manualized) CBT and usual care. They found that the modular condition demonstrated significantly steeper improvement trajectories than the standard or usual care conditions. Importantly, long-term outcomes revealed that therapists in the modular condition demonstrated greater satisfaction with evidence-based treatment than their counterparts in the standard CBT condition (Chorpita et al., 2013).

Transdiagnostic modular CBT treatments are transportable allowing for practice multiple settings (Friedberg et al., 2014). The transportability of transdiagnostic modular CBT is consistent with the ACA's aim to increase evidence-based practices at schools and pediatricians' offices where most children access mental health services. The ACA contains $200 million in funding for School-Based Health Centers (SBHCs) to promote health care prevention and screening protocols in school settings (Department of Health and Human Services, 2012a). However, dissemination and implementation of high quality SBHCs are difficult to achieve due to the unique challenges of the school schedule such as briefer sessions and school vacations (Weist et al., 2014). Transdiagnostic modularized treatment protocols offer flexibility in the selection of modules while continuing to adhere to the evidence-based literature providing for maximum effectiveness in a short period of time (Weist et al., 2014). Results implementing modular CBT programs in schools with anxious children (Chiu et al., 2013) and children with internalizing and externalizing problems (Chorpita et al., 2013) are promising. Longitudinally, results show the successful effects of modular CBT with clinically significant improvement for youth lasting from 6 months (Chorpita, Taylor, Francis, Moffitt, & Austin, 2004) to 1 year (Galla et al., 2012).

Transdiagnostic modular CBT is an effective treatment for a multitude of mental health disorders that currently flood pediatricians' and school counselors offices across the nation Training professionals to deliver accountable is an essential next step.

HARVESTING THE SEEDS OF CHANGE: DISSEMINATING THE APPROACH TO PRACTITIONERS

Transdiagnostic modular CBT fosters dissemination by requiring clinicians to learn fewer protocols in order to effectively address the problems their patients face. Further, clinicians may prefer an approach that embraces flexibility and clinical judgment. Multiple manuals overburden clinicians and complex procedures are less likely to be disseminated (Comer & Barlow, 2014). The transdiagnostic modular approach lessens the burden to the clinicians without sacrificing clinical integrity and potential effectiveness.

A transdiagnostic modular approach to clinician training is highly desirable, and indeed necessary, if we are to meet the growing demand for evidence-based treatments (EBT) and bridge the knowledge to practice gap (Kazdin, 2008). Unfortunately, advances in EBT development far outweigh any gains in training and dissemination methods, especially in children's mental health services (Lyon, Stirman, Kerns, & Bruns, 2011; Schoenwald, Hoagwood, Atkins, Evans, & Ringeisen, 2010; Ward-Zimmerman & Cannata, 2012). Indeed, access to efficacious treatments in community-based programs, heretofore, is currently not widespread because demand far outpaces the availability of trained practitioners (Becker & Stirman, 2011; Beidas, Koerner, Weingardt, & Kendall, 2011; Borntrager, Chorpita, Higa-McMillan, & Weisz, 2009; Schoenwald et al., 2010).

Technological advances offer much to support EBT implementation and dissemination with the capacity for large-scale training and knowledge sharing. Technology offers flexibility to reach large numbers of clinicians, researchers, clients, and other stakeholders in a highly cost-effective manner. These advances increase access to training and knowledge with tools that clinicians can use at any time, from any location. Furthermore, training that is scaled to meet the needs of clinicians at various levels of expertise across different settings create more efficient and effective systems of care (Beidas et al., 2011). Beidas et al. (2011) emphasized that technological advancements revolutionize the standard training approach beyond the traditional manual-style training and workshop approaches.

One promising approach to utilizing technology is to create training modules for each core competency and provide levels of training based on clinician skill and experience in a graduated fashion until mastery is achieved (Beidas et al., 2011). Beidas et al. (2011) described how their demonstration project for Behavioral Activation (BA) therapy was translated into an e-learning format. Blended e-learning models, when compared to traditional lecture approaches, offer the promise of enhanced learning, extensive and widespread dissemination, cost effectiveness and greater return on investment in training program development (Beidas, et al., 2011; Cucciare, Weingardt, & Villafranca, 2008).

The significance of practitioner's attitudes towards EBT's cannot be underestimated as the perception that evidence-based practices are restrictive and inflexible can influence decisions of adoptability and acceptability of these practices (Friedberg, Gorman, & Beidel, 2009; Nakamura et al., 2011). Borntrager and colleagues (2009) reported that therapists evaluated a modular-based approach more positively than a standardized manual approach. For instance, Borntrager et al. randomly assigned therapists to one of three training conditions: a standard manual treatment, a modular manual treatment, and treatment as usual. Results indicated that therapists' attitudes varied depending on the measures used, and that in general, therapists held positive attitudes toward modular treatment. Positive attitudes toward the modular approach likely stemmed from greater therapist involvement in decision-making. Interestingly, the treatments proposed in the modular approach did not differ from those offered in standard manuals, and most therapists in the modular approach, when presented with a clinical vignette, chose the same clinical technique indicated by standardized manual. Borntrager et al. concluded that in order to increase therapist buy-in, training formats need to be compatible across different treatment protocols and that training must address concerns about flexibility, therapeutic alliance, and clinical judgment. Training format can significantly influence therapist acceptance, and ultimately, their adoption of innovative and efficacious treatment practices in the field.

Training systems are needed to disseminate the best practices, lessons learned, as well as create partnerships between psychologists and primary care setting providers. These training systems need to be flexible, and adaptable to changing systems and contexts. The training ground is rich with potential to revolutionize treatment as usual by reaching not only mental health practitioners but also medical providers, including physicians and engaging practitioners to mentor interns, fellows, graduate students, and psychologists (Drotar, 2013; Pidano, Kimmelblatt, & Neace, 2011). Drotar (2013) emphasizes the need for creative models of collaboration and mentorship in a dynamic and changing landscape. For instance, Vogel et al. (2012) described a new training program aimed at enhancement of integrated care. In this program, psychology post-doctoral interns and medical residents trained together in an integrated primary care setting. Within this unique training experience, residents and interns "grow up" together as they are inundated in the practical application of skills. Budding practitioners share feedback with each other and demonstrate high levels of collaboration and communication.

Unfortunately, there are few professionals genuinely trained in CBT (Shafran et al., 2009). Some clinicians may "pose" as CBT-oriented practitioners and, subsequently, inadequately train others. Children suffer from this diluted dose of CBT and the CBT brand is sullied. Consequently, good training is essential in delivering a dose of CBT. Sburlati and colleagues (2012, 2014) delineated specific competencies for CBT with children and adolescents. They included abilities to understand CBT theory and research, develop a case formulation, engage in collaborative treatment with children and families, manage young patients' negative thoughts, help them change maladaptive behaviors, promote skill development, and modify dysfunctional family environments. However, measuring these competencies is a thorny issue.

The Cognitive Therapy Rating Scale (CTRS; Young & Beck, 1980) emerges as the gold standard for therapist evaluation. While the CTRS is widely used with both children and adults it does not assess several important competencies unique to doing effective CBT with youth. A new measure, the Cognitive Therapy Rating Scale for Children and Adolescents (CTRS-CA; Friedberg & Thordarson, 2013) is currently in development and addresses several features distinctive to CBT with young patients. Clearly, creation of reliable measures to assess CBT competence is a necessary future endeavor.

CONCLUSION

Runyan (2011, p. 66) recently asserted that clinicians should "seize the opportunity to position themselves at the forefront by not only responding but helping define the future of high quality cost-effective health care in the United States." Furthermore, it is critical for behavioral health care providers to demonstrate their value to the health care system to avoid having their services priced at the lowest cost point (Phelps, 2014; Rozensky, Tovian, & Sweet, 2014).

Bickman (2008, p. 437) astutely wrote, "Clinical care is a commodity, like barrels of oil that sell by the unit without regard to individual quality characteristics." Further, Bickman argued that when behavioral health services are viewed as such a commodity, they are naturally devalued and purchased at the lowest price point. Differentiation of services and ethical branding are ways to obviate commoditization. Simply, as behavioral health providers, we must assiduously avoid communicating that all clinical services are equally effective.

Kaslow, Graves, and Smith (2011) emphasized that contemporary consumers are drawn to specialized behavioral health services. Moreover, they added that access, quality improvement, accountability, continued parity, and patient centered health care homes all necessitate trained specialists. In order to improve the public's awareness of CBT and other evidenced-based practices, efforts must be directed at increasing mental health literacy. Potential consumers need to know what services are available, whether these services are genuinely evidenced based, and if the providers faithfully adhere to empirically established practices. Santucci, McHugh, and Barlow (2012) advocated for direct-to-consumer social marketing. They argued (p. 232), "Social marketing-or the application of commercial marketing science to programs designed to influence the behavior of the target audience to improve their personal welfare" is well-suited to increasing consumers' mental health literacy.

Public service announcements on radio and television, websites, social media, and community outreach all fit the bill for direct to consumer marketing. The About Our Kids radio program sponsored by the NYU Langone Medical Center (Dr. Radio, Sirius Channel 81) is a prime example of how electronic media can influence mental health literacy. Additionally, there are excellent websites by the American Psychological Association Division 53 (Clinical Child Psychology) (www.clinicalchildpsych.org) and the Help Your Keiki website (http://helpyourkeiki.com) (Nakamura et al., 2014).

Good training in modular CBT, on-going supervision and monitoring, verifying outcome data, and increasing the public's mental health literacy are ways to differentiate services and document accountability. To paraphrase Robert Frost, CBT is well-equipped to fulfill all these contemporary promises and yet has many more miles to go before all its goals are achieved. Greater research, more community outreach, and continued clinical model building will ensure a continuing place for behavioral health in the emerging health care environment.

REFERENCES

Asarnow, J., & Miranda, J. (2014). Improving care for depression and suicide risk in adolescents: innovative strategies for bringing treatments to community settings. *Annual Review Of Clinical Psychology*, *10,* 275-303. doi:10.1146/annurev-clinpsy-032813-153742

Bains, R., Franzen, C., & White-Fresé, J. (2014). Engaging african american and latino adolescent males through school-based health centers. *The Journal Of School Nursing: The Official Publication Of The National Association Of School Nurses*.

Becker, K. D., & Stirman, S.W. (2011). The Science of training in evidenced-based treatments in the context of implementation programs: Current status and prospects for the future. *Administration and Policy in Mental Health, 38,* 217-222. doi 10.1007/s10488-011-0361-0

Beidas, R., Koerner, K., Weingardt, K., & Kendall, P. (2011). Training research: practical recommendations for maximum impact. *Administration And Policy In Mental Health, 38*(4), 223-237. doi:10.1007/s10488-011-0338-z

Beidas, R. S., Stewart, R. E., Walsh, L., Lucas, S., Downey, M., Jackson, K., & ... Mandell, D. S. (2014). Free, brief, and validated: Standardized instruments for low-resource mental health settings. *Cognitive And Behavioral Practice*, doi:10.1016/j.cbpra.2014.02.002

Berwick, D. M., Nolan, T. W., & Whittington, J. (2008). The triple aim: Care, health, and cost. *Health Affairs, 27,* 759–769. doi:10.1377/hlthaff.27.3.759

Bickman, L. (2008). Why don't we have effective mental health services?. *Administration And Policy In Mental Health*, *35*(6), 437-439. doi:10.1007/s10488-008-0192-9

Black, M. M. (2002). Society of pediatric psychology presidential address: Opportunities for health promotion in primary care. *Journal of Pediatric Psychology*, *27*(7), 637-646. doi:10.1093/jpepsy/27.7.637

Borntrager, C. F., Chorpita, B. F., Higa-McMillan, C., & Weisz, J. R. (2009). Provider attitudes toward evidence-based practices: Are the concerns with the evidence or with the manuals. *Psychiatric Services*, *60*, 677-681. doi:10.1176/appi.ps.60.5.677

Chiu, A., Langer, D., McLeod, B., Har, K., Drahota, A., Galla, B., & ... Wood, J. (2013). Effectiveness of modular CBT for child anxiety in elementary schools. *School Psychology Quarterly: The Official Journal Of The Division Of School Psychology, American Psychological Association*, *28*(2), 141-153. doi:10.1037/spq0000017

Chorpita, B. F., Taylor, A. A., Francis, S. E., Moffitt, C., & Austin, A. A. (2004). Efficacy of modular cognitive behavior therapy for childhood anxiety disorders. *Behavior Therapy, 35*, 263–287. doi:10.1016/S0005-7894(04)80039-X

Chorpita, B., Weisz, J., Daleiden, E., Schoenwald, S., Palinkas, L., Miranda, J., & ... Gibbons, R. (2013). Long-term outcomes for the Child STEPs randomized effectiveness trial: a comparison of modular and standard treatment designs with usual care. *Journal Of Consulting And Clinical Psychology*, *81*(6), 999-1009. doi:10.1037/a0034200

Comer, J., & Barlow, D. (2014). The occasional case against broad dissemination and implementation: retaining a role for specialty care in the delivery of psychological treatments. *The American Psychologist*, *69*(1), 1-18. doi:10.1037/a0033582

Cucciare, M. A., Weingardt, K. R., & Villafranca, S. (2008). Using Blended Learning to Implement Evidence-Based Psychotherapies. *Clinical Psychology: Science & Practice*, *15*(4), 299-307. doi:10.1111/j.1468-2850.2008.00141.x

Cuthbert, B. N., & Insel, T. R. (2013). Toward the future of psychiatric diagnosis: the seven pillars of RDoC. *BMC Medicine*, *11*(1), 1-8. doi:10.1186/1741-7015-11-126

Departmentt of Health and Human Services (2012a). Affordable Care Act, from http://www.hhs.gov/opa/affordable-care-act/index.html

Department of Health and Human Services (2012b). Preventive Services Covered Under the Affordable Care Act, from http://www.hhs.gov /healthcare/facts/factsheets/2010/07/preventive-services-list.html

Department of Health and Human Services (2012c). The Affordable Care Act and the School-Based Health Center Capital Program, from http://www.hhs.gov/healthcare/facts/factsheets/2011/12/sbhc.html

Drotar, D. (2013). Reflections on clinical practice in pediatric psychology and implications for the field. *Clinical Practice In Pediatric Psychology*, *1*(2), 95-105. doi:10.1037/cpp0000017

Ehrenreich, J. T., Goldstein, C. R., Wright, L. R., & Barlow, D. H. (2009). Development of a unified protocol for the treatment of emotional disorders in youth. *Child & Family Behavior Therapy*, *31*(1), 20-37. doi:10.1080/07317100802701228

Friedberg, R., & Brelsford, G. (2011). Core principles in cognitive therapy with youth. *Child And Adolescent Psychiatric Clinics Of North America*, *20*(2), 369-378. doi:10.1016/j.chc.2011.01.009

Friedberg, R., Gorman, A., & Beidel, D. (2009). Training psychologists for cognitive-behavioral therapy in the raw world: a rubric for supervisors. *Behavior Modification*, *33*(1), 104-123. doi:10.1177/0145445508322609

Friedberg, R. D., Gorman, A. A., Hollar-Wilt, L., Biuckians, A., Murray, M., & Garcia, J. H. (2011). *Cognitive behavioral therapy for the busy child psychiatrist and other mental health professionals: Rubrics and rudiments*. New York, NY US: Routledge/Taylor & Francis Group.

Friedberg, R. D., Hoyman, L. C., Behar, S., Tabbarah, S., Pacholec, N. M., Keller, M., & Thordarson, M. A. (2014). We've come a long way, baby!: Evolution and revolution in CBT with youth. *Journal of Rational-Emotive & Cognitive-Behavior Therapy*, *32*(1), 4-14. doi:10.1007/s10942-014-0178-3

Friedberg, R. D., & Thordarson, M. A. (2013). *Cognitive therapy rating scale for child and adolescents.* Los Altos, CA: Center for the Study and Treatment of Anxious Youth.

Galla, B., Wood, J., Chiu, A., Langer, D., Jacobs, J., Ifekwunigwe, M., & Larkins, C. (2012). One-year follow-up to modular cognitive behavioral therapy for the treatment of pediatric anxiety disorders in an elementary school setting. *Child Psychiatry And Human Development, 43*(2), 219-226. doi:10.1007/s10578-011-0258-x

Garland, A., Haine-Schlagel, R., Brookman-Frazee, L., Baker-Ericzen, M., Trask, E., & Fawley-King, K. (2013). Improving community-based mental health care for children: translating knowledge into action. *Administration And Policy In Mental Health, 40*(1), 6-22. doi:10.1007/s10488-012-0450-8

Kaslow, N., Graves, C., & Smith, C. (2012). Specialization in psychology and health care reform. *Journal Of Clinical Psychology In Medical Settings, 19*(1), 12-21. doi:10.1007/s10880-011-9273-0

Kazdin, A. (2008). Evidence-based treatment and practice: new opportunities to bridge clinical research and practice, enhance the knowledge base, and improve patient care. *The American Psychologist, 63*(3), 146-159. doi:10.1037/0003-066X.63.3.146

Kelly, J. F., & Coons, H. L. (2012). Integrated health care and professional psychology: Is the setting right for you?. *Professional Psychology: Research & Practice, 43*(6), 586-595. doi:10.1037/a0030090

Kendall, P., Gosch, E., Furr, J., & Sood, E. (2008). Flexibility within fidelity. *Journal Of The American Academy Of Child And Adolescent Psychiatry, 47*(9), 987-993. doi:10.1097/CHI.0b013e31817eed2f

Kolko, D. J., & Perrin, E. (2014). The integration of behavioral health interventions in children's health care: Services, science, and suggestions. *Journal Of Clinical Child & Adolescent Psychology, 43*(2), 216-228. doi:10.1080/15374416.2013.862804

Lyon, A., R., Stirman, S. W., Kerns, S. E., & Bruns, E. J. (2011). Developing the mental health workforce: Review and application of training approaches from multiple disciplines. *Administration and Policy in Mental Health, 38*, 238-253. doi 10.1007/210488-010-0331-y

Nakamura, B. J., Chorpita, B. F., Hirsch, M., Daleiden, E., Slavin, L., Amundson, M. J., & ... Vorsino, W. M. (2011). Large-scale implementation of evidence-based treatments for children 10 years later: Hawaii's evidence-based services initiative in children's mental health.

Clinical Psychology: Science & Practice, *18*(1), 24-35. doi:10.1111/j.1468-2850.2010.01231.x

Nakamura, B. J., Mueller, C. W., Higa-McMillan, C., Okamura, K. H., Chang, J. P., Slavin, L., & Shimabukuro, S. (2014). Engineering youth service system infrastructure: Hawaii's continued efforts at large-scale implementation through knowledge management strategies. *Journal Of Clinical Child & Adolescent Psychology*, *43*(2), 179-189. doi:10.1080/15374416.2013.812039

Nash, J. M., Cubic, B. A., Khatri, P., & Baird, M. A. (2013). Essential competencies for psychologists in patient centered medical homes. *Professional Psychology: Research & Practice*, *44*(5), 331-342. doi:10.1037/a0033106

National Institute of Mental Health (2008). The national institute of mental health strategic plan. http://www.nimh.nih.gov/about/strategic-planning-reports/index.shtml

Nordal, K. C. (2012). Healthcare reform: Implications for independent practice. *Professional Psychology: Research & Practice*, *43*(6), 535-544. doi:10.1037/a0029603

North, S., McElligot, J., Douglas, G., & Martin, A. (2014). Improving access to care through the patient-centered medical home. *Pediatric Annals*, *43*(2), e33-e38. doi:10.3928/00904481-20140127-08

Phelps, R. (2014). The affordable care act and pediatric psychology. *Clinical Practice In Pediatric Psychology*, *2*(1), 99-100. doi:10.1037/cpp0000050

Pidano, A. E., Kimmelblatt, C. A., & Neace, W. P. (2011). Behavioral health in the pediatric primary care setting: Needs, barriers, and implications for psychologists. *Psychological Services*, *8*(3), 151-165. doi:10.1037/a0019535

Rozensky, R., & Janicke, D. (2012). Commentary: Healthcare reform and psychology's workforce: preparing for the future of pediatric psychology. *Journal Of Pediatric Psychology*, *37*(4), 359-368. doi:10.1093/jpepsy/jsr111

Rozensky, R., Tovian, S., & Sweet, J. (2014). Twenty years of the journal of clinical psychology in medical settings: we hope you will enjoy the show. *Journal Of Clinical Psychology In Medical Settings*, *21*(1), 1-9. doi:10.1007/s10880-014-9386-3

Runyan, C. N. (2011). Psychology can be indispensable to health care reform and the patient-centered medical home. *Psychological Services*, *8*(2), 53-68. doi:10.1037/a0023454

Santucci, L., McHugh, R., & Barlow, D. (2012). Direct-to-consumer marketing of evidence-based psychological interventions: introduction. *Behavior Therapy*, *43*(2), 231-235. doi:10.1016/j.beth.2011.07.003

Sburlati, E., Lyneham, H., Mufson, L., & Schniering, C. (2012). A model of therapist competencies for the empirically supported interpersonal psychotherapy for adolescent depression. *Clinical Child And Family Psychology Review*, *15*(2), 93-112. doi:10.1007/s10567-012-0111-1

Sburlati, E.S., Lyneham, H.J., Schniering, C.A., & Rapee, R.M. (2014). Evidence-based CBT for anxiety and depression in children and adolescents: A competencies based approach. New York: John Wiley.

Schoenwald, S. K., Hoagwod, K. E., Atkins, M. S., Evans, M. E., & Ringeisen, H. (2010). Workforce development and the organization of work: The science we need. *Administration and Policy in Mental Health*, *37*, 71-80. doi 10.1007/s10488-010-0278-z

Shafran, R., Clark, D., Fairburn, C., Arntz, A., Barlow, D., Ehlers, A., & Wilson, G. (2009). Mind the gap: Improving the dissemination of CBT. *Behaviour Research And Therapy*, *47*(11), 902-909. doi:10.1016/j.brat.2009.07.003

Sobel, A. B., Roberts, M. C., Rayfield, A. D., Barnard, M. U., & Rapoff, M. A. (2001). Evaluating outpatient pediatric psychology services in a primary care setting. *Journal of Pediatric Psychology*, *26*(7), 395-405. doi:10.1093/jpepsy/26.7.395

Tynan, W., & Woods, K. E. (2013). Emerging issues: Psychology's place in the primary care pediatric medical home. *Clinical Practice In Pediatric Psychology*, *1*(4), 380-385. doi:10.1037/cpp0000042

Vogel, M. E., Kirkpatrick, H. A., Collings, A. S., Cederna-Meko, C. L., & Grey, M. J. (2012). Integrated care: Maturing the relationship between psychology and primary care. *Professional Psychology: Research & Practice*, *43*(4), 271-280. doi:10.1037/a0029204

Ward-Zimmerman, B., & Cannata, E. (2012). Partnering with pediatric primary care: Lessons learned through collaborative colocation. *Professional Psychology: Research & Practice*, *43*(6), 596-605. doi:10.1037/a0028967

Warren, J., Nelson, P., Mondragon, S., Baldwin, S., & Burlingame, G. (2010). Youth psychotherapy change trajectories and outcomes in usual care: Community mental health versus managed care settings. *Journal Of Consulting And Clinical Psychology*, *78*(2), 144-155. doi:10.1037/a0018544

Weersing, V., Rozenman, M. S., Maher-Bridge, M., & Campo, J. V. (2012). Anxiety, depression, and somatic distress: Developing a transdiagnostic internalizing toolbox for pediatric practice. *Cognitive And Behavioral Practice*, *19*(1), 68-82. doi:10.1016/j.cbpra.2011.06.002.

Weist, M. D., Youngstrom, E. A., Stephan, S., Lever, N., Fowler, J., Taylor, L., & ... Hoagwood, K. (2014). Challenges and ideas from a research program on high-quality, evidence-based practice in school mental health. *Journal Of Clinical Child & Adolescent Psychology*, *43*(2), 244-255. doi:10.1080/15374416.2013.833097

Weisz, J. R., & Chorpita, B. F. (2012). 'Mod squad' for youth psychotherapy: Restructuring evidence-based treatment for clinical practice. In P. C. Kendall (Ed.), *Child and adolescent therapy: Cognitive-behavioral procedures (4th ed.)* (pp. 379-397). New York, NY US: Guilford Press.

Weisz, J., Chorpita, B., Palinkas, L., Schoenwald, S., Miranda, J., Bearman, S., & ... Gibbons, R. (2012). Testing standard and modular designs for psychotherapy treating depression, anxiety, and conduct problems in youth: a randomized effectiveness trial. *Archives Of General Psychiatry*, *69*(3), 274-282. doi:10.1001/archgenpsychiatry.2011.147

Wilamowska, Z., Thompson-Hollands, J., Fairholme, C., Ellard, K., Farchione, T., & Barlow, D. (2010). Conceptual background, development, and preliminary data from the unified protocol for transdiagnostic treatment of emotional disorders. *Depression And Anxiety*, *27*(10), 882-890. doi:10.1002/da.20735

Young, J., & Beck, A. T. (1980). Cognitive therapy scale: Rating manual. *Unpublished manuscript, University of Pennsylvania, Philadelphia*.

In: Cognitive Behavioral Therapy
Editor: Brendan Myers

ISBN: 978-1-63321-638-9

Chapter 2

TRAUMA FOCUSED COGNITIVE BEHAVIORAL THERAPY (TF-CBT) FOR CHILDREN WITH DEVELOPMENTAL DISABILITIES

Jenell Holstead, Ph.D.
and Jim Dalton, Psy. D., HSPP, CSAYC
University of Wisconsin – Green Bay
Damar Services, Inc.

ABSTRACT

Trauma-Focused Cognitive Behavioral Therapy (TF-BT) has strong empirical evidence of its effectiveness to treat Post-Traumatic Stress Disorder (PTSD) in children. Recently, some state licensing and oversight authorities have mandated that mental health providers use this protocol for children. Such mandates are often made without regard to diagnosis or intellectual functioning that might predict TF-CBT efficacy. However, no research has been conducted regarding the use of TF-CBT among the intellectually disabled population. Therefore, this study sought to fill this gap in the literature and determine if manualized TF-CBT was as effective as more traditional behaviorally based approaches. Results demonstrate that manualized TF-BT was less effective than behaviorally based approaches for children with cognitive disabilities. Implications of this research are discussed.

INTRODUCTION

Trauma-Focused Cognitive Behavioral Therapy (TF-CBT) is a psychosocial treatment model designed to address symptoms of Post-Traumatic Stress Disorder (PTSD) among children and adolescents. This treatment approach incorporates elements of cognitive-behavioral, interpersonal, attachment, humanistic, empowerment, and family therapy models. Developed in 2004 by Cohen, Deblinger, and Mannarino (2004), this treatment puts traumatic experiences into a broader context of the child's life to ensure the child's identity is not that of a victim. This therapy also resolves depressive and anxiety systems, and addresses distortions regarding self-blame, safety, and the dependability of others.

TF-CBT is implemented with children ages 3 to 18 and typically includes between 8 and 20 individual sessions (Cohen, Mannarino, & Deblinger, 2010). The duration of treatment may be extended for those with complex trauma to include up to 25 sessions depending on severity of symptoms (Cohen, Mannarino, Kliethermes, & Murray, 2012). The treatment includes education regarding PTSD symptoms, the cognitive triad (relationships between thoughts, feelings, and behaviors), individualized stress-management skills, safety skills, the creation of a trauma narrative (i.e., children gradually describe increasingly distressing details regarding the traumatic event),information regarding healthy sexuality, and in vivo desensitization. Overall, TF-CBT provides the opportunity for the child to develop appropriate coping skills and involves cognitive restructuring of maladaptive thoughts (Allen, Oseni, & Allen, 2012).

In addition to individual sessions, TF-CBT typically includes parents/guardians in the treatment regime. At the beginning, parents/guardians are seen separately and receive similar interventions that children receive along with parenting skills training. Towards the end of treatment, joint child-parent/guardian sessions are conducted to enhance communication regarding the traumatic event. However, it is important to note that adolescents can effectively receive TF-CBT treatment without the involvement of a parent/guardian (Black, Woodworth, Tremblay, & Carpenter, 2012).

TF-CBT has strong evidence of effectiveness to treat the symptoms of PTSD in children and adolescents (Allen et al., 2012; Cary & McMillen, 2012; Cohen & Mannarino, 2000; Deblinger, Stauffer, & Steer, 2001; Feather & Ronan, 2009; King et al. 2000). For example, King et al. compared a waitlist control condition to children receiving TF-CBT and found that those who had received TF-CBT significantly improved with regard to PTSD symptoms. In another study, children who received TF-CBT experienced greater reductions in PTSD symptoms and improvement on emotional and behavioral needs (Northwestern University Mental Health Services and Policy Program, 2008). In fact, Black et al. (2012) found TF-CBT to be effective at reducing trauma symptoms across different cultures and races, and it has been proved to be successful for both males and females. Moreover, TF-CBT appears to be more effective than other models of treatment (Cohen, Deblinger, Mannarino, & Steer, 2004; Cohen & Mannarino, 1996), with Black et al. strongly encouraging the use of this therapy to help youth reduce trauma-related symptoms. Therefore, TF-CBT is an evidenced-based treatment for children with traumatic experiences, and is an arguably better treatment than other therapies (Cohen et al., 2004).

TF-CBT for Children with Disabilities

In an attempt to ensure quality of service provided to children and adolescents who have experienced traumatic experiences, residential treatment providers in a Midwestern state are required by the Department of Child Services to provide TF-CBT. Children in residential care have experienced more physical and sexual abuse, as well as more failed placements (Heflinger, Simpkins, & Combs-Orme, 2000; Lyons, Kisiel, Dulcan, Cohen, & Chesler, 1997; Maunch, Krumholz, & Robinson, 2008; Walter, 2007;Zimmerman, 1994). A considerable amount of children also have difficult family relationships, and family histories of mental illness, domestic violence, and alcohol/drug abuse (Foltz, 2004; Frensch, 2002). Therefore, it is not surprising that a large amount of children referred to residential treatment have been diagnosed with PTSD (Maunch et al., 2008; Walter, 2007; Zimmerman, 1994). In fact, when the National Association for Children's Behavioral Health & the National Association of Psychiatric Health Systems surveyed residential treatment programs in 2007, 84% of residential treatment programs reported serving youth with PTSD (NACBH & NAPHS, 2008).

As children in residential care often have experienced trauma at a higher rate than other children, it is not surprising that residential treatment providers in a Mid-western state must collaborate with The National Child Traumatic Stress Network to insure that children with the highest levels of need have access to clinicians who have been suitably trained to address their complex issues. This mandate requires the use of TF-CBT for *all* children, including those that have cognitive disabilities. Despite strong evidence of effectiveness, the TF-CBT protocol has not been studied in populations with cognitive impairments or pervasive developmental disabilities. Instead, this protocol was developed to treat trauma symptoms specifically, without consideration for how to treat such symptoms alongside comorbid or co-occurring conditions, similar to most CBT protocols (Abramowitz, Franklin, & Cahill, 2003). In fact, most treatment protocols utilizing CBT are poorly suited for individuals with cognitive disabilities (Beail, 2003). Beail goes on to report that clinicians who adhere strictly to CBT treatment protocols in lieu of behavioral techniques may employ CBT techniques with limited success in populations with cognitive impairments.

Some modifications to CBT protocols, as well as additional treatment components, for individuals with limited cognitive functioning have been found to be effective. For example, Reaven and Hepburn (2003) describe modification including increased parental involvement in therapy, the inclusion of visual supports, and purposely incorporating the patient's unusual ideas and interests into treatment. In addition, simplified language and the use of modeling techniques in CBT treatment was beneficial for adults with developmental disabilities (Anderson & Morris, 2006). Overall, it is recommended that interventions be tailored to the unique needs of individuals to promote enhanced treatment outcomes (Pence, Aldea, Sulkowski, & Storch, 2011).

Need for the Study

At current, there is no research that examines the use of TF-CBT for children with cognitive disabilities. Numerous studies document the effectiveness of TF-CBT among children and report that TF-CBT takes into account a client's unique developmental level. Yet, no research has been conducted on the use of TF-CBT for youth with cognitive impairments. Guided treatment programs, such as TF-CBT, are sometimes criticized because of a lack of flexibility to meet the unique needs of client characteristics (especially those with multiple problems or diagnoses) (Allen et al., 2012).

Therefore, the purpose of this study was to examine whether TF-CBT is an effective treatment for children with coexisting trauma and cognitive disabilities. It was hypothesized that youth with cognitive disabilities who have experienced trauma would demonstrate less response to TF-CBT as compared to traditional behavioral-based and skill development training.

Method

A quasi-experimental study was conducted at Damar Services, Inc. to examine effectiveness of TF-CBT among children and adolescents with developmental and intellectual disabilities who have experienced trauma. Damar Services, Inc. is a private non-profit multi-site and multi-service agency located in Indianapolis, Indiana. The agency serves approximately 200 children in various residential care settings. Damar Services, Inc. specializes in treatment services for youth who have multiple and severe problems, including developmental and severe behavioral/emotional disorders. Traditionally, the average length of stay for children in traditional campus-based services is approximately 8 months.

Damar Services, Inc.'s milieu treatment model is based on Applied Behavior Analysis (ABA) approaches with individualized Intensive Behavioral Interventions (IBI) and skill building services. ABA/IBI treatment sessions at Damar Services are provided three times per week in a standardized format based on the child's treatment needs and symptoms including the completion of a Functional Behavioral Analysis (FBA). Behavioral interventions are designed and provided by a Masters level behavioral therapist and typically include repeated behavioral trials using backward behavioral chaining, discrete manipulation of variables, antecedent manipulations, positive reinforcement, compliance training, simple correction, extinction, teaching to specific adaptive skills, and over-correction, among other behaviorally-based interventions.

Participants

Participants in the study were selected from children referred to residential treatment services who had coexisting cognitive disabilities and trauma as measured by PTSD symptom presence. Participants were chosen from clients identified on the measure listed below as having elevations in PTSD symptoms. After the larger sample was identified, clients were assigned to one of two groups. Group A (Treatment Group) were children referred by the juvenile justice system – who were required by the state to be provided TF-CBT or other trauma-focused empirically-based treatment services (n=42). Group B (Control Group) were children referred by other funding sources like the Department of Education or the Bureau of Developmental Disabilities, and not required by contract to receive TF-CBT (n=45).

On average, Group A (Treatment Group) received three sessions of TF-CBT per week. During these sessions, ABA/IBI services were provided as necessary, but behaviorally based interventions were not the focus of the sessions, as the TF-CBT protocol was utilized. In contrast, Group B (Control Group) received three sessions per week of ABA/IBI interventions. Therefore, only Group A received TF-CBT, with Group A receiving far less ABA/IBI services due to the TF-CBT requirements. To the extent possible, subjects were matched between groups on gender, age, and degree of PTSD symptom elevation on the pretest measures.

Table 1 displays demographic information of children included in the current study. Of the 88 children included in the study, 18% were female and 81% were male.

Table 1. Demographics of Participants

	Treatment Group (TF-CBT)		*Control Group (no TF-CBT)*		*Total*	
Gender	*n*	%	*n*	%	*n*	%
Female	9	21%	7	16%	16	18%
Male	33	79%	38	84%	71	81%
Autism Diagnosis						
Yes	14	33%	16	35%	30	34%
No	28	66%	29	64%	57	65%
Total	**42**	--	**45**	--	**88**	--

The children ranged in age from 12 to 17 years. Each child included in the study was diagnosed with PTSD or had trauma-based symptoms, with all children in the study experiencing at least four, but not more than six adverse childhood experiences (ACEs).In addition to documented trauma, all children included in the study had mild cognitive disabilities, with intelligence scores ranging from 58-69 in the treatment group and 55-68 in the control group. Fourteen boys in the treatment group and sixteen boys from the control group had also been diagnosed with Autism.

While the control group and treatment group were referred for residential treatment by different sources, the differences in demographic and clinical presentation at admission between subject groups were minimal. The only significant difference noted was the average number of pre-admission juvenile justice contacts for the treatment group (2.5) which was greater than the control group (1.4). However, given the demographic and clinical matching between the groups, no treatment or response effects were hypothesized as a result of this difference.

Instruments

All participants were rated on levels of clinical symptoms using the Teacher Report Form of the Achenbach System of Empirically Based Assessment (ASEBA; Achenbach, 2001). Each participant's school teacher rated the participants internalizing and externalizing behaviors on a scale from "not true" to "very true". This assessment contains multiple scales including: Somatic, Withdrawn, Social Problems, Anxious/Depressed, Thought Problems, Attention Problems, Aggressive Behavior, and Rule Breaking. Higher scores in each of these domains represent higher symptomology. Teachers were 'blind' as to whether participants were in the TF-CBT group or ABA/IBI group. The ASEBA has been used in a substantial number of research studies and the scales are supported by a solid research base and are technically sound (Flanagan, 2005). This scale has been standardized on children between the ages of 6 and 18(Achenbach, 2001).

Procedures

The Teacher Report Form of the Achenbach was administered prior to the initiation of the study in December 2012. After this, clinicians implemented manualized TF-CBT (as required by state licensing) for the treatment group and ABA/IBI services for the control group. The Teacher Report Form of the Achenbach was then administered again in May 2013. T-scores for each of the subscales on the Achenbach and change scores (post minus pre) were calculated. Because higher scores on the Achenbach scales represent higher symptomology, it was expected that post-scores would be lower than pre-scores (as less symptomology should be present after therapy was provided).

Descriptive statistics were generated (means, standard deviations, frequency counts). Paired samples *t*-tests were used to compare the change between pre- and post-scores for the treatment and control groups. In addition, an independent sample *t*-test was used to compare the change-scores between the treatment and control groups. As the authors did not have any hypotheses that suggested the need to test for interactions, Repeated Measures ANOVAs were not utilized.

Table 2. Pre- and Post-Test Comparisons

	Treatment (TF-CBT) (n=42) M(SD)			Control (ABA/IBI services) (n=45) M(SD)			
Achenbach Subscale T-Scores	Pre	Post	Change	Pre	Post	Change	*Difference in Change***
Somatic	58.45(7.89)	57.45(7.84)	-1.00(5.68) p=.260	54.82(8.29)	53.71(6.56)	-1.11(4.97) p=.141	-0.111 p=.923
Withdrawn	60.55(8.75)	59.98(9.43)	-0.57(5.01) p=.465	61.33(8.36)	55.40(6.71)	-5.93(5.63) p=.000*	-5.362 p=.000***
Social Problems	65.02(9.11)	62.90(9.25)	-2.12(4.92) p=.008	66.58(9.11)	59.93(6.32)	-6.64(5.11) p=.000*	-4.525 p=.000***
Anxious/Depressed	68.26(7.66)	66.71(7.80)	-1.55(4.19) p=.021	66.29(9.21)	59.82(7.47)	-6.47(6.12) p=.000*	-4.919 p=.000***
Thought Problems	70.76(6.87)	69.00(6.57)	-1.76(4.32) p=.012	67.87(7.42)	61.47(6.27)	-6.40(4.59) p=.000*	-4.638 p=.000***
Attention Problems	71.12(6.83)	69.05(6.84)	-2.07(4.78) p=.008	71.98(8.81)	64.47(7.51)	-7.51(4.67) p=.000*	-5.440 p=.000***
Aggressive Behavior	72.64(5.47)	69.62(6.22)	-3.02(3.32) p=.000*	69.56(7.14)	62.40(5.94)	-7.16(4.26) p=.000*	-4.132 p=.000***
Rule Breaking	71.81(5.89)	70.02(4.72)	-1.79(3.69) p=.003*	63.04(6.69)	60.84(5.88)	-2.20(4.30) p=.001*	-0.414 p=.631

*Bonferroni Adjustment –family-wise error rate $p < .00625$.

**Difference is shown as control change minus treatment change (two-tailed t-test).

***Statistical significance at $p < .000$.

RESULTS

Results of the current study are presented in Table 2 and display the comparisons for the paired samples t-tests (comparing pre to post scores), as well as the independent sample *t*-test (comparing the change scores between the treatment and control groups). Because many *t*-tests were performed, a Bonferroni adjustment was calculated for the paired samples *t*-tests to prevent an inflated.

Type I error rate (Tabachnick & Fidell, 2007). Therefore, an adjusted family-wise *p* value of 0.00625 was used to determine significance for the paired samples *t*-tests.

A significant change from pre- to post-test was found in the control group for all subscales of the Achenbach with the exception of the Somatic subscale. For the other seven scales, a statistically significant difference between pre- and post-score was found and ranged from a 2.20 point decrease ($p = .001$) on the Rule Breaking subscale to a 7.51 point decrease ($p{=}.000$) on the Attention Problems subscale. As lower scores on the Achenbach represent less symptomology, decreases from pre- to post-test demonstrate decreased symptomology for seven of the Achenbach scales for the control group (ABA/IBI services). On the other hand, less change was observed for the TF-CBT treatment group.

Keeping the Bonferroni adjustment in mind, the only scales that showed significant change were the Aggressive Behavior subscale (change = -3.04, $p = .000$) and the Rule Breaking subscale (change = -1.97, $p = .003$).

In addition, a significant difference between the amount of change from pre- to post-test was also observed for six of the subscales on the Achenbach. Specifically, the control group significantly decreased in level of symptomology on average by 5.36 points ($p = .000$) on the Withdrawn scale, 4.525 points ($p = .000$) on the Social Problems subscale, 4.919 points ($p = .000$) on the Anxious/Depressed subscale, 4.638 points ($p = .000$) on the Thought Problems subscale, 5.440 points ($p = .000$) on the Attention Problems subscale, and 4.132 points ($p = .000$) on the Aggressive Behavior subscale as compared to the TF-CBT treatment group. In fact, across all subscales, the treatment group change was always a smaller decrease than that of the control group, with six subscales showing statistically significantly decreased symptomology. Therefore, these findings confirm the hypothesis: children with cognitive disabilities demonstrate less response to TF-CBT as compared to traditional ABA/IBI training.

Conclusion

The purpose of this study was to determine if TF-CBT was as effective for children with cognitive disabilities as other behaviorally based interventions. This study was necessary to determine if the empirical evidence supporting TF-CBT translated to those with intellectual disabilities. Results show that a manualized TF-CBT protocol (as required by the state's Department of Child Services) did not have as much benefit as ABA/IBI services for children with intellectual disabilities. As children with cognitive disabilities pose additional challenges to treating trauma, these results are not surprising. In fact, children with cognitive disabilities lack the capacity to learn and sustain new behaviors (Armour & Schwab, 2007). Therefore, ABA/IBI services (as opposed to cognitive based therapies) are more effective at treating trauma-related symptoms in this population.

Consistent with previous research, this study found that a standardized format should not be implemented for all clients, especially those with intellectual disabilities. The TF-CBT treatment model, like many other models, will better serve children with intellectual disabilities in a modified form. And, elements of TF-CBT can be used to enhance and add to ABA/IBI services for children with comorbid cognitive disabilities and trauma, as found in previous research. Allen et al. (2012) used an adapted TF-CBT model that was tailored to meet the unique needs of the client successfully and advocated that clinicians use clinical judgment within the parameters of a treatment model. In fact, protocol developers typically recommend that treatment not be implemented in a standardized format, with clinicians strongly urged to monitor treatment and modify as necessary (Amaya-Jackso & DeRosa, 2007). Therefore, states and other regulatory bodies must recognize that each unique child has quite diverse needs. As such, mandating the use of a standardized protocol without regard for child responsivity variables is not advised.

The current study is not without limitations that must be acknowledged. First, subjects were matched between groups on basic demographics to the extent possible. However, this is problematic as the groups were not exactly the same across all dimensions. In addition, there were only 88 participants in the study, a relatively small sample size. Second, random assignment was not used to determine who would receive the TF-CBT as compared to the ABA/IBI group. Because certain youth referred for residential care were required by the state to be provided with TF-CBT, these youth made up the TF-CBT group. Other children (referred by the Department of Education or Bureau of Developmental Disabilities) formed the control group, as they were not required to be provided with TF-CBT. It is possible that the type of student referred from each organization differed, impacting the results of the study. Lastly, other instruments may have provided more information on specific trauma-related symptoms. Although the Achenbach Teacher Report Form includes subscales regarding anxiety and thought problems, other instructions may have provided more information on PTSD symptomology specifically.

TF-CBT has strong evidence of its effectiveness. However, attention must be paid to the child's intellectual functioning when providing CBT based intervention models aimed at symptom reduction. In some cases, modifications should be made to tailor treatment to each child's unique needs. Outside of intellectual disabilities, other childhood conditions are implicated when considering the use of mandated protocols. For example, children who have comorbid trauma experiences and severe mental illness, traumatic brain injury, and autism spectrum disorders, among other conditions, also may be less responsive to TF-CBT. Therefore, the present study should inform and impact local, state, and federal policies regarding mandated protocol use.

REFERENCES

Abramowitz, J. S., Franklin, M. E., & Cahill, S. P. (2003).Approaches to common obstacles in the exposure-based treatment of obsessive–compulsive disorder. *Cognitive and Behavioral Practice, 10,* 14–22.

Achenbach, T.M. (2001). *Manual for the ASEBA School-Age Forms & Profiles.* Burlington, VT: University of Vermont.

Allen, B., Oseni A., & Allen, K. E. (2012). The evidence-based treatment of chronic posttraumatic stress disorder and grief in an adolescent: A case study. *Psychological Trauma: Theory, Research, Practice, and Policy, 4* (6), 631-639. doi:10.1037/a0024930.

Amaya-Jackson, L., & DeRose, R. R. (2007). *The diagnostic and statistical manual of mental disorders-text revision* (4th ed.). Washington, DC: Author.

Armour, M. P. & Schwab, J. (2007). Characteristics of difficult-to-place youth in state custody: A profile of the exceptional care pilot project population. *Child Welfare, 86*(3), 71-96.

Beail, N. (2003). What works for people with mental retardation? Critical commentary on cognitive—behavioral and psychodynamic psychotherapy research. *Mental Retardation, 41,* 468–472.

Black, P. J., Woodworth, M., Tremblay, M., & Carpenter, T. (2012). A review of trauma-informed treatment for adolescents. *Canadian Psychology, 53*(3), 192-203. doi:10.1037/a0028441

Cary, C. E., & McMillen, J. C. (2012). The data behind the dissemination: A systematic review of trauma-focused cognitive behavioral therapy for use with children and youth. *Child and Youth Services Review, 34,* 748–757. doi:10.1016/j.childyouth.2012.01.003

Cohen, J. A., Deblinger, E., & Mannarino, A. (2004). Trauma-focused cognitive behavioral therapy for sexually abused children. *Psychiatric Times, 21*(9), 52-53.

Cohen, J. A., Deblinger, E., Mannarino, A. P., & Steer, R. A. (2004). A multisite, randomized controlled trail for children with sexual abuse-related PTSD symptoms. *Journal of American Academy of Child & Adolescent Psychiatry, 43*, 393-402. doi:10.1097/07481180802440209

Cohen, J. A., & Manarino, A. P. (1996). A treatment outcome study for sexually abused preschool children: Initial findings. Journal of the American Academy of Child & Adolescent Psychiatry, 35, 42-50. doi:10.1097/00004583-199601000-00011

Cohen, J. A., Mannarino A. P. (2000). Predictors of treatment outcome in sexually abused children. *Child Abuse Neglect, 24*(7), 983-994.

Cohen, J. A., Mannarino, A. P., & Deblinger, E. (2010). Trauma-focused cognitive- behavioral therapy for traumatized children. In J. R. Weisz & A. E. Kazdin (Eds.), *Evidence-based psychotherapies for children and adolescents* (2nd ed., pp. 295–311). New York, NY: Guilford Press.

Cohen, J. A., Mannarino, A. P., Kliethermes, M., & Murray, L. A. (2012). Trauma-focused CBT for youth with complex trauma. *Child Abuse and Neglect, 36,* 528-541.

Deblinger, E., Stauffer, L. B., Steer, R. A. (2001). Comparative efficacles of supportive and cognitive behavioral group therapies for young children who have been sexually abused and their nonoffending mothers. *Child Maltreat,* 6(4), 332-343.

Feather, J. S., & Ronan, K. R. (2009). Trauma-focused CBT with maltreated children: A clinic based evaluation of a new treatment manual. *Australian Psychologist, 44,* 174 –194. doi:10.1080/00050060903147083

Flanagan, R. (2005). The Achenbach system of empirically based assessment. In J. Impara & B. Plake (Eds.), The *Sixteenth Mental Measurements Yearbook* (pp. 9-17). *Lincoln*, NE: Buros Institute of Mental Measurements.

Foltz, R. (2004). The efficacy of residential treatment: An overview of the evidence. *Residential Treatment for Children & Youth, 22* (2), 1-19.

Frensch, K.M. & Cameron, G. (2002). Treatment of choice or a last resort ? A review of residential mental health placements for children and youth. *Child & Youth Care Forum, 31* (5), 307- 339.

Heflinger, C. A., Simpkins, C. G., & Combs-Orme, T. (2000). Using the CBCL to determine the clinical status of children in state custody. *Children and Youth Services Review, 2,* 55-73.

King, N. J., Tonge, B. J., Mullen, P., Myerson, N., Heyne, D., Rollings, S., Martin, R., & Ollendick, T. H. (2000). Treating sexually abused children with posttraumatic stress symptoms: A randomized clinical trial. *Journal of the American Academy of Child Adolescent Psychiatry*, 39(11), 1347-1355.

Lyons, J. S., Kisiel, C. L., Dulcan, M., Cohen, R., & Chesler, P. (1997). Crisis assessment and psychiatric hospitalization of children and adolescents in state custody. *Journal of Child and Family Studies, 6,* 311-320.

Maunch, D., Krumholz, A., & Robinson, G. (2008). *Characteristics of residential treatment: For children and youth with serious emotional disturbances.* Abt Associates, Inc.

National Association for Children's Behavioral Health (NACBH) and the National Association of Psychiatric Health Systems (NAPHS). (2008). Characteristics of Residential Treatment for Children and Youth with Serious Emotional Disturbances. Cambridge, MA: Abt Associates, Inc.

Northwestern University Mental Health Services and Policy Program. (2008). *Evaluation of the implementation of three evidence-based practices to address trauma for children and youth who are wards of the state of Illinois* (Final report). Northwestern University, Chicago.

Pence, S. L., Aldea, M. A., Sulkowski, M. L., & Storch, E. A. (2011). Cognitive behavioral therapy in adults with Obsessive-Compulsive Disorder and Borderline Intellectual Functioning: A case of series of three patients. *Journal of Developmental Physical Disabilities (23),* 71-85. doi: 10.1007/s10882-010-9200-6

Reaven, J., & Hepburn, S. (2003). Cognitive-behavioral treatment of obsessive–compulsive disorder in a child with Asperger syndrome. *Autism, 2,* 145–164.

Tabachnick, B. G., & Fidell, L. S. (2007). *Using Multivariate Statistics.* Boston: Pearson.

Walter, U. M. (2007). *Residential treatment: A review of the national literature.* State of Kansas Department of Social and Rehabilitation Services.

Zimmerman, P. (1994). A pilot demographic study of population changes in a residential treatment center. *Residential Treatment for Children & Youth, 11,* 17-33.

In: Cognitive Behavioral Therapy
Editor: Brendan Myers

ISBN: 978-1-63321-638-9

Chapter 3

COGNITIVE BEHAVIORAL THERAPY FOR INFORMAL CANCER CAREGIVERS: A REVIEW OF THE LITERATURE AND FUTURE DIRECTIONS

Mia S. O'Toole[1], Douglas S. Mennin[2], Megan E. Renna[2], Robert Zachariae[1,3] and Allison J. Applebaum[4,*]

[1]Department of Psychology and Behavioral Sciences, School of Business and Social Sciences, Aarhus University, Aarhus, Denmark

[2]Department of Psychology, CUNY Hunter College and the Graduate Center, New York, US

[3]Unit for Psychooncology and Health Psychology, Aarhus University and Aarhus University Hospital, Aarhus, Denmark

[4]Department of Psychiatry and Behavioral Sciences, Memorial Sloan Kettering Cancer Center, New York, US

ABSTRACT

The experience of providing care to a loved one with cancer is associated with significant psychological, physical, temporal, and

[*] Correspondence should be addressed to Allison Applebaum, Ph.D. Assistant Attending Psychologist, Department of Psychiatry and Behavioral Sciences, Memorial Sloan Kettering Cancer Center, 641 Lexington Avenue, 7th Floor, New York, New York 10065. Tel.: (646) 888 – 0034. E-mail: applebaa@mskcc.org.

financial burden. A growing number of interventions have been developed to address the psychological component of burden among informal cancer caregivers (ICs), of which cognitive behavioral therapies (CBTs) have shown particularly promising results. No overall synthesis of CBTs for ICs exists, and the present chapter therefore provides a systematic review of previous studies of CBTs for ICs, their target outcomes, therapeutic components, and effects. We conclude that although our knowledge of the burden experienced by caregivers has increased over the past decade, this knowledge has not yet been sufficiently translated into effective interventions for caregivers. Informed by recent advances in the affective sciences, this chapter presents emotion regulation as an important target for future interventions. We argue that the distress experienced by ICs can be conceptualized as products of maladaptive regulation of the motivational and emotional conflicts associated with providing care. Based on this model, recommendations for future CBT interventions are provided.

Introduction

Cancer rates are increasing globally (World Cancer Research Fund International, 2014) resulting not only in a growing number of cancer patients, but also informal caregivers (ICs), defined as any relatives, friends, or partners who have a significant relationship with and provide assistance (i.e., instrumental, emotional) to a patient with a medical illness (Hudson & Payne, 2009). In 2009, 65,700,000 people in the United States served as ICs for medically ill relatives, including 4,600,000 cancer patients (National Alliance for Caregiving, 2009). Increased rates of survival, combined with shorter hospital stays and advanced home care technology, have led to a shift in care and an increase in the number of untrained and unsupported ICs of patients with cancer (Jemal et al., 2011, National Alliance for Caregiving, 2009, Siegel et al., 2012).

Caregiver Burden

Numerous studies have described the many detrimental effects of providing care for others, with the overall message being that caregiving adversely affects multiple domains of quality of life for this population (for overviews see Romito, Goldzweig, Cormio, Hagedoorn, & Andersen, 2013; Stenberg, Rulan, & Miaskowski, 2010). The burden experienced by ICs is multifaceted and is associated with psychological, physical, temporal, and financial demands. For example, ICs experience a number of psychological complaints, including internal distress such as symptoms of anxiety and depression. Between 10 and 53% of ICs report clinically significant symptoms of depression, and approximately 16-56% report clinically significant symptoms of anxiety (Askari, Madgaonkar, & Rowell, 2012; Braun, Mikulincer, Rydall, Walsh, & Rodin, 2007; Clavarino, Lowe, Carmont, & Barlanda, 2002; Cliff & MacDonagh, 2000; Hudson, Thomas, Trauer, Remedios, & Clarke, 2011; Janda et al., 2008; McLean, Walton, Matthew, & Jones, 2011; Mellon, Northouse, & Weiss, 2006). Research has shown that symptoms of anxiety and depression may be as high (Baider et al., 1996; Ferrario, Zotti, Massara, & Nuvolone, 2002; Given et al., 1993; Given et al., 2006; Kornblith, Herr, Ofman, Scher, & Hollands, 1994; Cliff & MacDonagh, 2000; Kris et al., 2006; Rivera, 2009) or even higher in ICs than in patients themselves (Askari et al., 2012; Baider & Kaplan De-Nour, 1988; Braun et al., 2007; Cliff & MacDonagh, 2000; Gallagher, Parle, & Cairns, 2002; McLean et al., 2011; Vanderwerker, Laff, Kadan-Lottick, 2005). Above symptom report, a sizeable group of ICs meet clinical criteria for psychological disorders, the most common of which are adjustment disorders and major depression (Akechi et al., 2006). Although the majority of current research has relied on cross-sectional methods, the few existing longitudinal studies show that caregiver burden is significantly associated with anxiety and depression over time (Butow, Price, Bell, Webb, & deFazio, 2014; Girgis et al., 2013; Kim, Shaffer, Carver, & Cannady, 2014). Such psychopathology persists into survivorship, as 30-40% of caregivers continue to experience symptoms above clinical threshold levels of anxiety and depression if their loved one survives cancer (Lambert, Gigis, Lecathelinais, & Stacey, 2013; Lambert, Jones, Gigis, & Lecathelinais, 2012). Furthermore, the caregiving role has been associated with a range of physical health complications (e.g., Burton, Newsom, Schulz, Hirsch, & German, 1997; Given & Given, 1992; Given et al., 2004), including sleep difficulties (Carter, 2003; Cho, Dodd, Lee, Padilla, & Slaughter, 2006; Hearson & McClement, 2007), fatigue (Jensen & Given, 1991; Teel & Press, 1999), cardiovascular disease (Lee, Colditz, Berkman, & Kawachi, 2003; von Känel et al., 2008; Vitaliano et al., 2002), poor immune functioning (Kiecolt-Glaser et al., 1987; Pariante et al., 1997; Rohleder, Marin, Ma, & Miller, 2009; Scanlan, Vitaliano, Zhang, Savage, & Ochs, 2001; Vitaliano et al., 1998), and increased mortality (Christakis & Allison, 2006; Schulz & Beach, 1999). Caregiving also involves significant demands on time, and data from a 2009 survey of caregivers in the United States showed evidence that, on average, cancer caregivers provided care for 8.3 hours each day for 13.7 months (Yabroff & Kim, 2009). Finally, a greater number of caregiving hours has been associated with work productivity loss (Mazanec, Daly, Douglas, & Lipson, 2011) and thus introduces a financial challenge. Indeed, ICs represent one of the most critical elements of the healthcare system in the United States today (National Alliance for Caregiving, 2009).

Cognitive Behavioral Therapies

Cognitive behavioral therapies (CBTs) are effective in treating individuals presenting with symptoms of anxiety and depression (Hofmann, Asnaani, Vonk, Sawyer, & Fang, 2012; Hofmann & Smits, 2008), although treatment gains do not appear very durable in cases of comorbid anxiety and depression (Hofmann et al., 2012; Newman, Przeworski, Fisher, & Borkovec, 2010). For ICs specifically, previous reviews of psychological interventions have produced rather mixed results and effect sizes have been of small to medium magnitudes (e.g., Applebaum & Breitbart, 2013; Northouse, Katapodi, Song, Zhang, & Mood, 2010). Interventions including cognitive-behavioral therapeutic components have fared the best (Applebaum & Breitbart, 2013; Sörensen, Pinquart, & Duberstein, 2002), and CBT appears to be an appropriate first-choice for ICs in need of psychosocial intervention. Therefore, in light of the extensive psychological burden experienced by ICs, and the potential for CBTs to ameliorate this element of burden, a greater understanding of the specific ways in which CBTs target burden is critical. In the present chapter, we present a narrative, systematic review of existing CBTs for ICs. Our primary aim is to describe and evaluate the characteristics and targets of the interventions. Based on our review of study findings, we discuss strengths and limitations of current CBTs for ICs and provide recommendations for future investigations.

Methods

Search Strategy

We conducted a systematic review of all CBTs for ICs of cancer patients from the earliest time available through January 2014. We electronically searched PubMed, PsychINFO, Cochrane, CINAHL, and Embase using the following search terms: To target cancer, we used *cancer, oncology, palliative care, palliative medicine, neoplasm,* and *malignancy*. Caregivers were identified by the search terms *caregiver(s) and caregiving,* while CBT was targeted by *intervention, coping skills, psychosocial, problem-solving, iCBT, CBT, cognitive therapy, behavioral intervention, cognitive intervention, home practice, eHealth, cognitive restructuring, exposure, mindfulness, meditation, relaxation training, cognitive behavior therapy, cognitive behavioral therapy, online therapy, online treatment, internet treatment, internet-based therapy, psychotherapy*. Two independent searches were conducted by the first (MSO) and third author (MR).

Inclusion Criteria

The studies included in the present review all investigated the effect of CBT for adult ICs (mean age $\geq$ 18 years). An intervention was considered a CBT if it included at least of one of the following components: cognitive restructuring, imaginal or in vivo exposure, coping skills training, problem-solving, behavior activation, behavioral experiments, structured homework, acceptance-based strategies, stress and anxiety management through relaxation, or mindfulness (cf. Nenova et al., 2013). Additionally, included studies employed at least one quantitative measure of psychological, physical, or social functioning of the IC pre and post intervention. Only studies reported in English language peer-reviewed journals were included. All papers were evaluated independently by MSO and MR, and disagreement on the inclusion/exclusion of a study was resolved by consensus.

Study Description

All included studies were evaluated descriptively. We examined study sample characteristics, including demographic (mean age and gender distribution) and clinical (cancer diagnosis and cancer stage of the patient for whom the IC provided care) variables. Study characteristics such as outcome measures used (e.g., quality of life, anxiety), and study design (i.e., randomization, control conditions) were also evaluated. Furthermore, interventions were evaluated based on CBT components used (e.g., cognitive restructuring, mindfulness), the mode of delivery (e.g., in-person or technology-based) and provider type (e.g., nurse or psychologist). Finally, the dose and duration of the interventions were described.

RESULTS

Search Results

Information flow and study selection is provided in Figure 1. The searches produced a total of 1,526 articles. After duplicates were removed, 1,047 abstract were screened, and 79 full-texts were retrieved and evaluated, resulting in 23 included studies. Included papers and 11 relevant reviews/meta-analyses identified in the search were screened for additional studies. This produced an additional 84 studies that were evaluated, of which 16 met inclusion criteria. In total, 39 studies fulfilled the inclusion criteria, of which 20 studies were included following consensus ratings. Two studies (Harden et al., 2009; Northouse et al., 2007) described the same sample, and were therefore collapsed and described as a single result. Reasons for exclusion are listed in Figure 1.

Study Characteristics

Table 1 presents an overview of included studies. Studies were primarily conducted with participants from North America (N=33). Three studies were conducted in Europe, two in Australia, and one in Israel. A total number of 5,172 ICs were examined. ICs were predominately white (85% to 100%), female (31%-100%), and on average between 48 and 63 years old. Twenty studies specified the relationship between the cancer patient and caregiver, with the most common relationship being the patient's spouse/partner (46%-100%). A large proportion of studies included caregivers of patients with multiple cancers (N=25). Regarding stage of disease, ICs provided care for patients with advanced cancer (stage III to IV; N=14), early stage cancer (stage I to II; N=7), and survivors (N=3). Fifteen studies reported mixed stages of disease or did not report any information on stage.

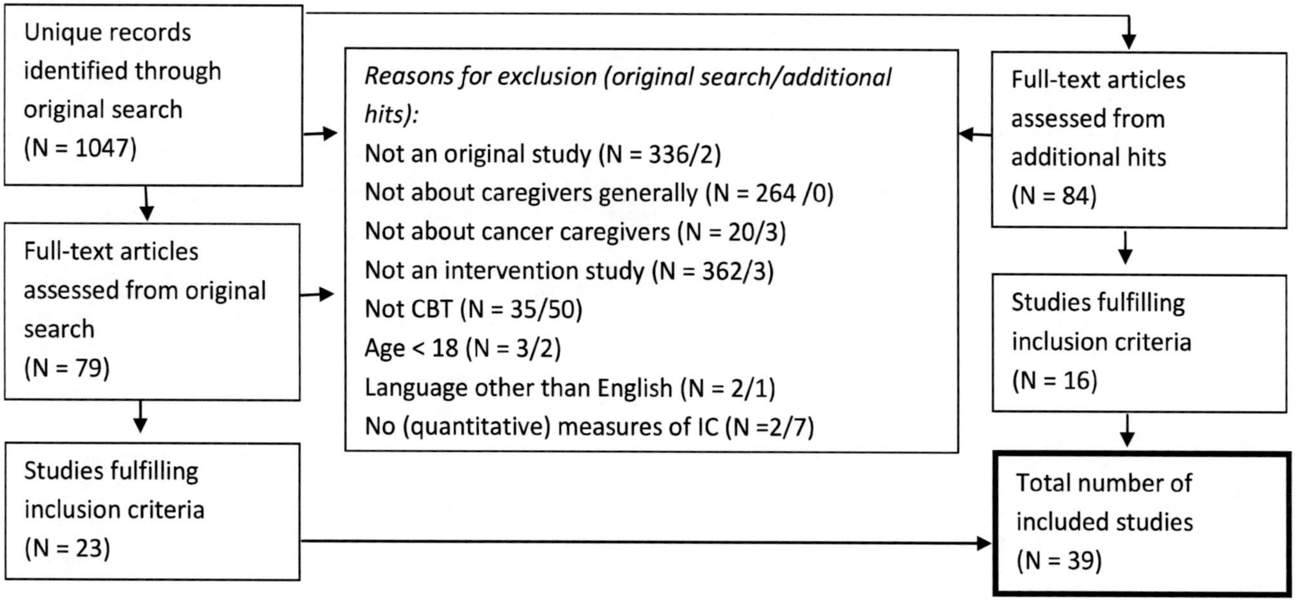

Figure 1. Flow chart of study selection.

Table 1. Characteristics of the 39 included studies

Study (country)	Intervention type & main components	Study design (control group), dose, & duration	Outcome measures	Interventionist; Delivery mode	Sample size. Attrition	Demographic characteristics of sample. (Relationship)	Clinical characteristics of sample Results	Results
Baucom et al., 2009 (USA)	Couple-based relationship enhancement; standardized Components: Problem solving Homework assignments	RCT; 2 arm (control: TAU). Pre-post-12 month follow-up design 6 sessions delivered biweekly for 75 minutes	4 outcomes: Quality of marriage (QMI) Sexual functioning (DISF-SR) Psychological distress (BSI-18) Posttraumatic growth (PGI)	Advanced doctoral students in clinical psychology; in person	Total $N = 15$ couples 9 in intervention Attrition = 11% pre intervention	Median age= 50 86% white 100% men (100% married/ partnered)	Breast cancer, early stage	No inferential statistics due to small sample
Bevans et al., 2010 (USA)	Problem-solving education model; individualized dyadic intervention Components: Problem solving Cognitive restructuring	OT (no control) Pre-post and follow-up design 4 sessions delivered pre HCST, at discharge, & 2 and 4-weeks post discharge	3 outcomes: Psychological distress (BSI) Problem solving (Social problem-solving inventory) Symptom distress: (SDS)	Clinical nurse specialist, nurse scientist, or licensed independent clinical social worker; in person	Total $N = 10$ dyads 10 (5 dyads) in intervention Attrition = 20% during or post intervention	Mean age= 54 62.5% female 87.5% white, non-Hispanic (100% married/ partnered)	Mixed types of cancer, stage unknown	No inferential statistics due to small sample
Bevans et al., 2013 (USA)	Problem-solving education for patient/caregiver team; standardized Components: Problem solving	OT (no control) Pre-post design 3 1-hour sessions over 3 weeks	2 outcomes: Self-efficacy (CSES), Psychological distress (BSI-18)	Nurses or social workers; delivered either through phone or in person	Total $N = 195$ (113 ICs) Attrition = 11% pre, 28 % during intervention	Mean age= 53 72.2% female 77.8% white	Allogeneic hematopoietic stem cell transplant patients, advanced stage	Improved self-efficacy & distress

Study (country)	Intervention type & main components	Study design (control group), dose, & duration	Outcome measures	Interventionist; Delivery mode	Sample size. Attrition	Demographic characteristics of sample. (Relationship)	Clinical characteristics of sample Results	Results
Birnie et al., 2010 (Canada)	Mindfulness-Based Stress Reduction for couples; standardized Components: Mindfulness	OT (no control) Pre-post design 8 weeks, 90 minute sessions	3 outcomes: Mood disturbance (POMS; 6 subscales) Stress (C-SOSI; 8 subscales) Mindfulness (MAAS)	No interventionist information provided; in person	Total $N = 41$ couples Attrition = 49 % during intervention	Mean age= 63 52.4% female	Mixed cancer types, early stage	Significant effect of intervention on mood disturbance & mindfulness
Blanchard et al., 1996 (USA)	Problem-solving intervention (Coping with Cancer); individualized Components: Problem solving	RCT; 2 arms (control: usual care). Pre-post-follow-up design 6 weeks of 1-hour sessions	9 outcomes: Perceived health status (SF20; 6 subscales) State anxiety (STAI) Depression (CES-D) Marital adjustment (DAS) Satisfaction with social support (HDFL) Coping behavior (ICRs; 3 subscales) Stress (related to 17 typical caregiver problems and 3 most pressing problems) Coping (with 17 problems and 3 most pressing problems)	Oncology social worker; in person	Total $N = 66$ 30 in intervention Overall attrition= 23%	Mean age= 55 60% female 100% white (100% married/ partnered)	Mixed cancer types, stage unknown	No significant group*time interaction effects of intervention

Table 1. (Continued)

Study (country)	Intervention type & main components	Study design (control group), dose, & duration	Outcome measures	Interventionist; Delivery mode	Sample size. Attrition	Demographic characteristics of sample. (Relationship)	Clinical characteristics of sample	Results
Budin et al., 2008 (USA)	Telephone counseling (TC), with or without standardized psychoeducation (combo-group); individualized Components: Appraisal Coping skills	RCT; 4 arms (control: disease management (DM)/DM plus psychoeducation) Pre-post design 4 sessions	5 outcomes: Psychological well-being/Emotional adjustment (PAL-C) Overall health (SRHS) Vocational environment (PAIS) Social environment (PAIS) Domestic environment (PAIS)	Nurse; telephone based	Total N =249 dyads 66 in TC, 58 in combo-group Attrition for TC = 36% pre and 29% during intervention Attrition for combo-group = 17% pre and 40% during intervention	Mean age= 52 41.6% female 70.4% white (68% married/ partnered)	Breast cancer, mixed stages	No between-group differences
Cameron et al., 2004 (Canada)	Brief problem-solving intervention; standardized Components: Problem solving	OT (no control) Pre-follow-up design 1 hour session	4 outcomes: Problem solving (SPSI-SF; 6 subscales) Emotional well-being (POMS; 7 subscales) Assistance provided (CAS) Self-efficacy (CSES)	No interventionist; tech-based slide presentation	Total N = 71 Attrition = 18% pre, 19% during, and 17% post intervention	Mean age= 54 68% women (73.5% married/ partnered)	GI and lung cancer, advanced stage	Improvements over time in the emotional tension subscale of POMS
Campbell et al., 2006 (USA)	Coping skills training; standardized	RCT; 2 arms (control: usual care) Pre-post design	3 outcomes: Self-efficacy (SESCI; 4 subscales) QOL (POMS-SF; 6	Doctoral-level medical psychologists; telephone	Total N = 40 dyads 20 in intervention	Mean age= 58	Prostate cancer, survivors	No between-group effects

Study (country)	Intervention type & main components	Study design (control group), dose, & duration	Outcome measures	Interventionist; Delivery mode	Sample size. Attrition	Demographic characteristics of sample. (Relationship)	Clinical characteristics of sample	Results
	Components: Problem solving Relaxation Coping skills Cognitive restructuring	6 1-hour phone calls	subscales) Caregiver strain (CSI)	based	Attrition = 40% during intervention			
Canada et al., 2005 (USA)	CBT for dyads; Standardized Components: HW assignments Skills training	RCT; 2 arm (control: same treatment for patient only) Pre-post and follow-up design 4 sessions; 1st session 60-90 minutes, 2nd-4th sessions 45-60 minutes each	3 outcomes: Sexual function (FSFI) Marital adjustment (DAS) Psychological distress (BSI)	PhD clinical psychologist or Masters level counselor; in person	Total $N = 51$ couples 25 in dyad group Overall attrition= 40% during intervention, 25% post intervention	Mean age= 62 100% women 88% white (100% married/ partnered)	Prostate cancer, 3 or 5 year survivors	A significant effect of time on sexual function/satisfaction on FSFI
Carter, 2006 (USA)	Caregiver sleep intervention; individualized Components: Relaxation	RCT; 2 arms (control: information and training about body mechanics) Pre-post-follow-up design 2 1-hour sessions over 5 weeks	4 outcomes: Sleep-quality (PSQI) Depression (CES-D) QOL (CQOLC) Sleep logs and actigraphical monitoring (3 variables)	Master's level research nurses; in person	Total $N = 30$ 15 in intervention Attrition = 14% pre, 0% during and post intervention	Mean age= 52 66% female 87% white (67% married/ partnered)	Mixed cancer types, advanced stage	No time*group interaction effects reported, but ICs showed greater improvements in PSQI scores at each time point

Table 1. (Continued)

Study (country)	Intervention type & main components	Study design (control group), dose, & duration	Outcome measures	Interventionist; Delivery mode	Sample size. Attrition	Demographic characteristics of sample. (Relationship)	Clinical characteristics of sample	Results
Chih et al., 2012 (USA)	Comprehensive Health Enhancement Support System (CHESS) with online clinical reports (CR); standardized Components: Coping skills Problem solving	RCT; 2 arms (control: CHESS without CR) Pre-follow-up design User driven on-demand	3 outcomes: Preparedness (FCI) Physical burden (CBI) Negative mood (POMS)	No interventionist; web-based	Total $N = 217$ 110 in intervention Attrition = 9% pre intervention, 49% during follow-up	Mean age = 56 65% female 92 % white (69% married/ partnered)	Mixed cancer types, advanced stage	No overall effect of time reported
Christensen, 1983 (USA)	Couples Treatment Program; individualized Components: Problem solving Positive reappraisal	RCT; 2 arms (control: not described) Pre-post design 4 sessions	8 outcomes: Marital happiness LWMAS) Sexual satisfaction (SSS) Depression (BDI) Self-esteem (RSS) Helplessness (ILCS) Anxiety (STAI) Discomfort (PSI) Alienation (PSI)	Therapist; in person	Total $N = 20$ couples 10 in intervention Attrition: N/A	No demographic information provided.	Breast cancer, early stage	Significant between-group difference on sexual satisfaction & discomfort
Clark et al., 2006 (USA)	Multidisciplinary intervention; standardized Components:	RCT; 2 arms (control: standard medical care) Pre-post-follow-up design	2 outcomes: QOL (LASA) Caregiver burden (interview)	Psychologist or psychiatrist; in person	Total $N = 83$ 43 in intervention	69 over age 50 72% female (89% married/ partnered)	Mixed cancer types, advanced stage	No between-group effects

Study (country)	Intervention type & main components	Study design (control group), dose, & duration	Outcome measures	Interventionist; Delivery mode	Sample size. Attrition	Demographic characteristics of sample. (Relationship)	Clinical characteristics of sample	Results
	Coping skills Relaxation	8 90-minute sessions over 3 weeks			Attrition: N/A			
Clark et al., 2013 (USA)	Multidisciplinary intervention; standardized Components: Relaxation Problem solving Coping	RCT; 2 arms (control: standard care) Pre-post-follow-up design 6 sessions, 90 minutes each over 4 weeks. 10 brief telephone-based conseling sessions during follow-up.	1 outcome: QOL (CQOLI-C)	Multidisciplinary interventionists; in person	Total $N = 117$ 65 in intervention Attrition= 17% during, 5% post intervention	Mean age and gender: N/A (79% married/ partnered)	Mixed cancer types, advanced stage	Between-group difference at post only (4 weeks)
Cohen & Kuten, 2006 (Israel)	Cognitive-behavioral group intervention; standardized Components: Relaxation Cognitive restructuring Reframing Problem solving Homework assignments	OT; 2 groups (control: standard psychosocial care) Pre-post-follow-up design 9 sessions of 90 minutes each	4 outcomes: Adjustment (PAIS) Psychological distress and global severity (BSI) Sleep (MSQ) Social Support (MSPSS)	Senior social worker; in person	Total $N = 143$ 80 in intervention Attrition = 35% during intervention	Mean age= 53 69.2% female (46.2% married /partnered)	Mixed cancer types (40.4% breast), stage unknown	Significant time*group interaction effects on all 4 outcomes

Table 1. (Continued)

Study (country)	Intervention type & main components	Study design (control group), dose, & duration	Outcome measures	Interventionist; Delivery mode	Sample size. Attrition	Demographic characteristics of sample. (Relationship)	Clinical characteristics of sample	Results
DuBenske et al., 2013 (USA)	Comprehensive Health Enhancement Support System (CHESS); standardized Components: Coping skills Problem solving	RCT; 2 arms (control: internet information) Pre-and bimonthly assessment for 24 months User driven on-demand	3 outcomes: Disruptiveness (CQOLI-C) Burden (CQOLI-C) Negative mood (POMS)	No interventionist; web/tech based	Total $N = 246$ 144 in CHESS group Attrition= 14% pre intervention	Mean age= 56 68.3% female (72% married/ partnered)	Lung cancer, advanced stage	Significant between-group effects at 6 months on burden and negative mood
Fegg et al., 2013 (Germany)	Existential Behavior Therapy; standardized Components: Mindfulness Stress management	RCT; 2 arms (control: TAU). Pre-post-follow-up design 6 group sessions totaling 22 hours	2 outcomes: Psychological distress (BSI; 3 subscales) QOL (3 measures: SWLS, QOL-NRS, WHOQOL-BREF)	Behavioral therapists; in person	Total $N = 160$ 81 in intervention Attrition= 15% during, 4% post intervention	Mean age= 55 69.9% female	Palliative care patients (83% with cancer diagnosis), mixed cancer types	Significant between-group effects on anxiety and all QOL scales at post and long-term follow-up assessment
Given et al., 2006 (USA)	Cognitive-behavioral modeled intervention; individualized Components: Traditional/full CBT	RCT; 2 arms (control: TAU) Pre-post design 10 sessions; 5 in person and 5 via phone over 20 weeks	1 outcome: Reaction to assistance (author-derived measure)	Registered nurse; in person and telephone based	Total $N = 237$ 118 in intervention Attrition = 28% during intervention	Mean age= 55 55.1% female (65% married/ partnered)	Mixed cancer types, mixed stages	Significant effect of intervention at 10 weeks (mid treatment)

Study (country)	Intervention type & main components	Study design (control group), dose, & duration	Outcome measures	Interventionist; Delivery mode	Sample size. Attrition	Demographic characteristics of sample. (Relationship)	Clinical characteristics of sample	Results
Heinrich & Schag, 1985 (USA)	Stress and activity management (SAM) program; standardized Components: Relaxation Problem solving Homework assignments	OT: 2 groups (TAU) Pre-post-follow-up design 6 weeks; 2 hours per session	7 outcomes: Fund of information (Cancer Information Test) Adjustment (PAIS) Daily activities (Daily activity diary) Anxiety, depression, and global severity (SCL-90-R) QOL (author-derived measure)	Clinical psychologists; in person	Total $N = 25$ 12 in intervention Overall attrition = 31% during intervention	No demographic information provided.	Mixed cancer types, stage unknown	Significant time*group interaction effect showing increased fund of information in SAM
Kayser et al., 2010 (USA)	Partners in Coping Program; standardized Components: Relaxation	RCT; 2-arm (control: Social work services) Pre-post and follow-up design 9 biweekly hour long sessions	2 outcomes:QOL (QOL) Illness intrusiveness (IIRS)	Clinical social worker; in person	Total $N = 63$ 36 couples in intervention Attrition = 25% during, 4% post intervention	Mean age= 49 90% white (87.2% married/partnered)	Breast cancer, early stage.	No significant time*group effects

Table 1. (Continued)

Study (country)	Intervention type & main components	Study design (control group), dose, & duration	Outcome measures	Interventionist; Delivery mode	Sample size. Attrition	Demographic characteristics of sample. (Relationship)	Clinical characteristics of sample	Results
Keefe et al., 2005 (USA)	Partner-guided pain management; standardized Components: Coping skills	RCT; 2 arms (control: usual care) Pre-post design 3 sessions; 45-60 minutes each	3 outcomes: Self-efficacy (CPSS; 3 subscales) Caregiver strain (CSI) Mood (POMS; 2 indexes)	Registered nurse; in person	Total $N = 78$ 41 in intervention Attrition = 32% post intervention	Mean age= 59 61.8% female 79% white	Mixed cancer types, advanced stage	Between-group differences on 2 subscales of self-efficacy at post
Kogler et al., 2013 (Germany)	Existential Behavior Therapy ; standardized Components: Mindfulness	RCT; 2 arms (control: TAU) Pre-post-follow-up design 6 group sessions; 22 hours total	4 outcomes: Mindfulness (CAMS-R, FFMQ) Psychological distress and global severity (BSI) QoL (WHOQOL-Bref) Satisfaction with life (SWLS)	Psychotherapists; in person	Total $N = 160$ 73 in intervention (80,8% ICs) Overall attrition= 15%	No demographic information provided	Mixed cancer types, palliative stage	No between-group comparisons
Kuijer et al., 2004 (Holland)	Brief Counseling program; standardized Components: Cognitive restructuring	RCT; 2 arms (control: wait list) Pre-post-follow-up design 5 biweekly sessions-	3 outcomes: Depression (CES-D) Relationship quality (Likert-scale) Investment and benefit(author-derived measure)	Psychologist; in person	Total $N = 59$ couples 31 in intervention Attrition = 3% pre, 19 % during,	Mean age= 49 70% female (90% married/ partnered)	Mixed cancer types, stage unknown	Curvelinar effects showing lower levels of perception of underinvest-ment/over-benefit, higher

Study (country)	Intervention type & main components	Study design (control group), dose, & duration	Outcome measures	Interventionist; Delivery mode	Sample size. Attrition	Demographic characteristics of sample. (Relationship)	Clinical characteristics of sample	Results
	HW assignments	90 minutes each			23% post intervention			overinsvestment /underbenefit, and higher relationship quality from pre to post intervention maintained throughout follow-up Results are not specific to ICs
Kurtz et al., 2005 (USA)	Cognitive-behavioral intervention; individualized Components: Coping skills	RCT; 2 arms (control: conventional care) Pre-mid-post design 10 sessions (5 in person, 5 via phone) over 20 weeks	4 outcomes: Depression (CES-D), Social functioning (SF-36) Caregiver involvement (total number of assistance) Mastery (author-derived measure)	Nurse; in person and telephone based	Total N = 237 118 in intervention Overall attrition= 24% between pre and mid, 22% between mid and post intervention	Mean age= 55.2 55.6% female 94% white	Mixed cancer types, mixed stages	No between-group effects

Table 1. (Continued)

Study (country)	Intervention type & main components	Study design (control group), dose, & duration	Outcome measures	Interventionist; Delivery mode	Sample size. Attrition	Demographic characteristics of sample. (Relationship)	Clinical characteristics of sample	Results
Lengacher et al., 2012 (USA)	Mindfulness-Based Stress Reduction; standardized Components: Mindfulness Stress reduction	OT (no control) Pre-mid-post design 6 weeks (3 in person, 3 audiotaped sessions)	5 outcomes: QOL (MOS-SF) Perceived stress (PSS) Psychological distress (anxiety and depression; (CES-D, STAI) Stress and inflammatory markers (cortisol and IL-6) Physical & psychological symptoms (MSAS)	Licensed clinical psychologist; in person & via audiotape	Total $N = 26$ dyads Attrition= 12% at post intervention	Mean age= 51.5 61.5% female 88.5% white (84.6% married/ partnered)	Mixed cancer types, advanced stage	No between-group statistics reported. No within-group effects of intervention over time on total scores
Manne et al., 2004 (USA)	Psychoeducational group intervention; standardized Components: Stress management Coping skills Relaxation	RCT; 2 arms (control: no treatment) Pre-post design 6 weeks	5 outcomes: Psychological distress (MHI) Cancer specific distress (IES) Coping (COPE; 4 subscales) Post traumatic growth (PTGI; 5 subscales) Marital	Multidisciplinary team; in person	Total $N = 68$ 33 in intervention Attrition= 12% at post	Mean age= 59.6 84% white 100% female	Prostate cancer, mixed stages	Significant between-group effects showing improved coping (pos reappraisal, denial, & emotional approach), & post traumatic

Study (country)	Intervention type & main components	Study design (control group), dose, & duration	Outcome measures	Interventionist; Delivery mode	Sample size. Attrition	Demographic characteristics of sample. (Relationship)	Clinical characteristics of sample	Results
			communication (Communication patterns questionnaire)					growth (relation to others, personal growth, spirituality, appreciation for life) in intervention group
Manne et al., 2011 (USA)	Intimacy-Enhancing Therapy; standardized Components: Skill building HW assignments	RCT; 2-arm (control: usual care) Pre-post design 5 sessions 90 minutes each	6 outcomes: Psychological functioning (PDS) Psychological wellbeing (PWS) Cancer specific distress (IES) Cancer concerns (authors-derived measure) Relationship functioning (DAS) Relationship intimacy (PAIR)	Psychotherapist; in person	Total *N* = 71 couples 37 in intervention Attrition= 22% during intervention	Mean age= 60 100% female (100% married /partnered)	Prostate cancer, survivors	No between-group effects

Table 1. (Continued)

Study (country)	Intervention type & main components	Study design (control group), dose, & duration	Outcome measures	Interventionist; Delivery mode	Sample size. Attrition	Demographic characteristics of sample. (Relationship)	Clinical characteristics of sample	Results
McMillan et al., 2005 (USA)	Coping Skills Intervention (COPE Model); standardized Components: Positive reframing	RCT; 3 arms (control: usual hospice care/ usual hospice care plus supportive visits) Pre-post-follow-up design 1 week intervention; 3 visits, 1st visit 45 minutes, 2nd & 3rd 30 minutes each	4 outcomes: QOL (CQOL-C) Symptom burden (MSAS) Task burden & mastery (CDS)	Nurse; in person	Total $N = 328$ 111 in COPE group Attrition =7% pre, 28% during and post intervention	Mean age= 63.1 76.6% female	Mixed cancer types, advanced stage	Group*time effect of intervention for CG task burden & symptom burden, favoring COPE
Meyers et al., 2011 (USA)	Cognitive-behavioral problem-solving educational intervention (COPE Model); standardized Components: Problem solving	RCT; 2 arms (control: usual care) Pre-post-follow-up design 3 sessions	2 outcomes: QOL (CHQLI) Problem-solving skills (SPSI-R)	Health educators; in person	Total $N = 476$ dyads 348 in intervention Attrition = 3% pre, 48% during intervention	31% female 85% white (70% married/partnered)	Mixed cancer types, advanced stage	Significant between-group effect of intervention on QOL
Northouse et al., 2005 (USA)	Family Intervention (FOCUS); standardized Components:	RCT; 2 arms (control: usual care) Pre-follow-up design	5 outcomes: Appraisal (ACS) Uncertainty (MUIS) Hopelessness (BHS) Coping (BRIEF	Master's level nurse; in person & telephone based	Total $N = 182$ couples 94 in intervention	Mean age= 52 77% white (62% married/partnered)	Breast cancer, advanced stage	Group*time effect of intervention on negative appraisal

Study (country)	Intervention type & main components	Study design (control group), dose, & duration	Outcome measures	Interventionist; Delivery mode	Sample size. Attrition	Demographic characteristics of sample. (Relationship)	Clinical characteristics of sample	Results
	Positive reappraisal	5 sessions	COPE; 2 subscales) Mental and Physical QOL (scale derived from FACT and SF-36)		Attrition= 27% at follow up			
Northouse et al., 2007/ Harden et al., 2009 (USA)	Family Intervention (FOCUS); standardized Components: Positive reappraisal	RCT; 2 arms (control: standard care) Pre- and follow-up design 5 sessions (3 90 minute sessions in person, 2 30 minute sessions by phone)	7 outcomes: QOL (MOS SF-12, FACT-G; 3 subscales) Appraisal (ACS) Uncertainty (MUIS) Hopelessness (BHS) Coping resources (BCO; 3 subscales) Self-efficacy (LCSES) Symptom distress (EPIC)	Nurse; in person & telephone based	Total $N = 263$ dyads 129 in intervention Attrition = 12% pre, 10% during and post intervention	Mean age= 59 84% white	Prostate cancer, mixed stages	Significant between-group effect of intervention only at 4 month follow-up on QOL (FACT-G, SF mental health), appraisal, & coping (self-efficacy and communication scales)

Table 1. (Continued)

Study (country)	Intervention type & main components	Study design (control group), dose, & duration	Outcome measures	Interventionist; Delivery mode	Sample size. Attrition	Demographic characteristics of sample. (Relationship)	Clinical characteristics of sample	Results
Northouse et al., 2013 (USA)	Brief FOCUS Intervention and Extensive FOCUS Intervention; standardized Components: Positive reappraisal	RCT; 3 arms (control: usual care) Pre-post design Brief: 3 sessions, 2 90-minute home visits and 1 30-minute phone call. Extensive: 6 sessions, 4 90-minute home visits & 2 30-minute phone calls. Both 10 weeks in duration	9 outcomes: QOL (Functional assessment of cancer therapy; 4 subscales) Appraisal (AIS) Uncertainty (MUIS) Hopelessness (BHS) Coping (Brief COPE; 2 subscales) Healthy behaviors (author-derived measure) Self-efficacy (LCSES) Dyadic support (SSQ) Communication(LMIS)	Nurses; in person & telephone based	Total $N = 484$ dyads 99 in brief and 99 in extensive FOCUS Overall attrition= 38% during and post intervention	Mean age= 56.7 55.8% female 82.5% white (74% married/ partnered)	Mixed cancer types, advanced stage	Group*time effect of intervention on overall coping, self-efficacy, and social QOL, favoring extensive FOCUS Results not specific to ICs
Porter et al., 2009 (USA)	Partner-assisted emotional disclosure; standardized Components:	RCT; 2 arms (control: education/support). Pre-post design	4 outcomes: Marriage quality (QMI) Intimacy (MSIS) Psychological	Master's level psychologist or social worker; in person	Total $N = 130$ couples 65 in intervention	Mean age= 59.3 82% white 71% female	GI cancer, mixed stages	Between-group analyses showed that intervention improved

Study (country)	Intervention type & main components	Study design (control group), dose, & duration	Outcome measures	Interventionist; Delivery mode	Sample size. Attrition	Demographic characteristics of sample. (Relationship)	Clinical characteristics of sample	Results
	Skills training	4 in person-sessions (1st session 75 minutes, 2nd-4th sessions 45 minutes) over 8 weeks maximum	distress (POMS-SF) Holding back (modified questionnaire)		Attrition = 26% during intervention			relationship quality with no differences between patients and ICs in ITT analysis. In completer analysis, intimacy increased for patients only
Porter et al., 2011 (USA)	Coping Skills Training; standardized Components: Relaxation Cognitive reappraisal Problem solving	RCT; 2 arms (control: education/support) Pre-post-follow-up design 14 telephone-based sessions (tapered from weekly, biweekly, to monthly)	3 outcomes: Psychological distress (POMS-B) Caregiver strain (CSI) Self-efficacy (modified CPSS)	Registered nurses; telephone based	Total $N = 233$ 117 in intervention Attrition = 31% during, 20 post intervention	Mean age= 59.3 69% female 82% white	Lung cancer, mixed stages	No between-group effects

Table 1. (Continued)

Study (country)	Intervention type & main components	Study design (control group), dose, & duration	Outcome measures	Interventionist; Delivery mode	Sample size. Attrition	Demographic characteristics of sample. (Relationship)	Clinical characteristics of sample	Results
Reele, 1994 (USA)	I Can Cope Program or I Can Cope w/ ongoing support group; individualized Components: Relaxation Stress reduction Coping skills	OT; 3 groups (control: did not receive either intervention) Pre-post design 8 weekly 2-hour sessions	2 outcomes: QOL (QOLI) Coping strategies (author-derived measure)	Oncology clinical nurse specialist; in person	Total $N = 32$ 12 in I Can Cope, 8 in I Can Cope + support intervention Attrition: N/A	No demographics provided	Mixed cancer types, stages unknown	No between-group effects
Schover et al., 2012 (USA)	Web-based (WEB)& face-to-face (FF) counseling about regaining erections and sexual satisfaction (CAREss); standardized Components: HW assignments Cognitive reframing Belief identification	RCT; 3 arms (control: wait list). Pre-post-follow-up design 3 sessions over 12 weeks (session 1 90 minutes, 2nd & 3rd sessions 50-60 minutes)	3 outcomes: Sexual function (FSFI) Psychological distress (BSI-18) Dyadic adjustment (DAS)	Therapist; web based or in person	Total $N = 163$ couples 60 in FF and 55 in WEB intervention Attrition FF = 28% during, 7% post intervention. Attrition WEB = 13% during, 17% post intervention	(100% married/ partnered) No demographics reported	Prostate cancer, early stage	No between-group effects
Scott et al., 2004 (Australia)	Couples-based coping training (CanCOPE); standardized	RCT; 3 arms (control: medical education (ME) or ME plus	4 outcomes: Communication (6 behaviors identified via video recordings)	Female, registered psychologists; in person &	Total $N = 94$ couples n in intervention:	Mean age= 53 98% white (91% married/ partnered)	Breast or gynecological cancer, early stage	No significant group*time effect of intervention

Study (country)	Intervention type & main components	Study design (control group), dose, & duration	Outcome measures	Interventionist; Delivery mode	Sample size. Attrition	Demographic characteristics of sample. (Relationship)	Clinical characteristics of sample	Results
	Components: Reappraisal Problem solving Coping skills	supportive counseling). Pre-post and follow-up design 5 2-hour sessions & 2 30-minute phone calls	Coping (RWCQ-C) Psychological distress (PAIS-SR; 2 subscales) Sexual difficulties (PAIS-SR)	telephone-based	N/A Overall attrition =10 % during, 30% post intervention			
Scott & Beatty, 2013 (Australia)	Internet-based cognitive behavioral therapy; standardized Components: Coping skills Relaxation	OT (no control) Pre-post- follow up design 6 weeks	2 outcomes: Cancer sistress & negative affect (DASS, PSDSS) QOL (EORT-QLC; 4 subscales)	No interventionist; web based	Total $N = 13$ Attrition= 31% during intervention	Mean age= 48.9 66.7% female (66.7% married/ partnered)	Mixed cancer types, early stage	No inferential statistics due to small sample.

Table 1. (Continued)

Study (country)	Intervention type & main components	Study design (control group), dose, & duration	Outcome measures	Interventionist; Delivery mode	Sample size. Attrition	Demographic characteristics of sample. (Relationship)	Clinical characteristics of sample	Results
Toseland et al., 1995 (USA)	Coping with Cancer Intervention; standardized Components: Problem solving reappraisal	RCT; 2 arms (control: usual care) Pre-post design 6 1-hour sessions	13 outcomes: Depression (CES-D) Anxiety (STAI) Marital satisfaction (DAS) Satisfaction with social (HDLF; 1 subscale)) Health status (MOS SF20; 6 subscales) Burden (ZBI; objective and subjective) Help seeking (HSCI; 4 subscales) Coping (ICR; 3 subscales) Presence of and coping with "Pressig problems" (rating of 17 problems) Caregiving mastery (LCACS) Caregiving satisfaction (LCACS) Drug and alcohol use (HDLF; 1 subscale)	Social worker; in person	Total $N = 86$ 44 in intervention Overall attrition= 9% during intervention	Mean age= 56 50% female 100% white	Mixed cancer types, unknown stage	No significant group*time effect of intervention

Note: ACS= Adjustment to Cancer Scale; BFI= Brief Fatigue Inventory; BHS= Beck Hopelessness Scale; BPI= Brief Pain Inventory; BSI= Brief Symptom Inventory; C-SOSI= Calgary Symptoms of Stress Inventory; CAMS-R= Cognitive and Affective Mindfulness Scale-revised; CAS= Caregiver Assistance Scale; CBI= Caregiver Burden Inventory; CDS= Caregiver Demands Scale; CES-D= Center for Epidemiologic Studies Depression Scale; CHQLI= City of Hope Quality of Life Instrument; CPSS= Chronic Pain Self-Efficacy Scale; CQOLI-C= Caregiver Quality of Life- Cancer Scale; CSES= Caregiver Self-Efficacy Scale; CSI= Caregiver Strain Index; DAS= Dyadic Adjustment Scale; DISF-SR= Derogatis Inventory of Sexual Functioning; EORTC-QLQ= European Organization for Research and Treatment of Cancer Quality of Life Core Questionnaire; EPIC= Expanded Prostate Cancer Index Composite; FACT-B= Functional Assessment of Cancer Therapy; FACT-G= Functional Assessment of Cancer Treatment; FCI= Family Care Inventory; CBI= Caregiver Burden Inventory; FFMQ= Five Facet Mindfulness Questionnaire; FSFI= Female Sexual Function Index; HDLF= Health and Daily Living Form; ICR= Index of Coping Resources; IES; Impact of Event Scale; IIEF= International Index of Erectile Dysfunction; IIRS= Illness Intrusiveness Rating Scale; ILCS: Internal Locus of Control Scale; LASA= Linear Analog Self-Assessment; LCACS= Lawton Caregiving Appraisal Composite Scale; LCSES= Lewis Cancer Self-Efficacy Scale; LMIS= Lewis Mutuality and Interpersonal Sensitivity Scale; LWMAS= Locke-Wallace Marital Adjustment Scale; MAAS= Mindful Attention Awareness Scale; MHI= Mental Health Inventory; MOS-SF-12= Medical Outcomes Study 12-item; short form; MSIS= Miller Social Intimacy Scale; MSPSS= Multidimensional scale of perceived social support; MSQ= Mini Sleep Questionnaire; MUIS= Mishel Uncertainty in Illness Scale; OT= Open Trial; PAIR= Personal Assessment of Intimacy in Relationships; PAIS= Psychosocial Adjustment to Illness Scale; PDS= Psychological Distress Scale; PGI= Posttraumatic Growth Inventory; POMS(-SF)= Profile of Mood States (short form); PSDSS= Posttraumatic Stress Disorder Symptom Scale; PSQI= The Pittsburgh Sleep Quality Index; PSS= Perceived Stress Scale; PWS= Psychological Well-being Scale; QMI= Quality of Marriage Inventory; QOL= Quality of Life; QOL-NRS= Quality of Life- Numeric Rating Scale; QOLI= Quality of Life Inventory; RCT= Randomized Control Trial; RSC= Rotterdam Symptom Checklist; SCL-90-R= Symptom Checklist- 90- Revised; RSS= Rosenberg Self-Esteem Scale; RWCQ-C= Revised Ways of Coping Questionnaire – Cancer Version; SDS= Symptom Distress Scale; SESCI= The Self-Efficacy for Symptom Control Inventory; SF-20= Medical Outcomes Study- 20 item; SF-36= Short Form Health Survey; SIS= Self-image Scale; SPSI-R= Social Problem-Solving Inventory- Revised; SPSI-SF= The Social Problem-Solving Inventory- short form; SRHR= Self-rated Health subscale; SSS= Sexual Satisfaction Scale; STAI= State Trait Anxiety Inventory; SWLS= Satisfaction with Life Scale; WHOQOL-BREF= World Health Organization Quality of Life- brief form; ZBI= Zarit Burden Interview.

Most interventions were delivered in person only (N=23), while a few were delivered over the phone (N=3) or Internet (N=4). Nine interventions used multiple delivery modes. According to our definition of CBT presented above, 25 studies included two or more CBT components. CBT components used included: reappraisal/reframing/cognitive restructuring (N=16), problem solving (N=15), coping skills training (N=13), relaxation (N=12), homework assignments (N=7), stress management (N=5), mindfulness (N=3), communication skills training (N=3), and belief identification (N=1). Number of sessions varied between one and 15, except for some web-based interventions that were user-driven and therefore not delivered in confined sessions.

Attrition rates refer to the proportion of individuals allocated to an intervention but who either did not initiate treatment or dropped out prior to completion of the post-intervention assessment. We have specified whether attrition occurred during or post intervention in the intervention group(s). If attrition rates specific to the intervention group were unavailable, the overall attrition rate is noted in Table 1. Attrition was reported in 34/39 studies (87%), and attrition during intervention was reported in 21/34 studies (62%). During intervention, attrition ranged from 0%-49%. No clear patterns emerged regarding associations between attrition and treatment components, delivery mode, or characteristics of ICs/patients.

Of the 39 included studies, 31 were randomized controlled trials (RCTs) and three were multi-armed open trials (OTs). Twenty-seven studies had one control group, five had two control groups, and one had three control groups. Most studies used a control group receiving standard care/treatment as usual (N=22), which in two cases included unspecified psychosocial care. Eleven studies used an active control group (e.g., psychoeducation) or a limited version of the treatment under investigation (e.g., without a hypothesized crucial treatment component). Six studies were one-armed OTs and did not include a control group. One RCT included a control group with cancer patients only (Canada, Neese, Sui, & Schover, 2005) and results for the IC group were therefore uncontrolled.

The number of outcome measures is included in Table 1, and if specified by the authors, only primary outcome measures are noted. The outcomes varied greatly, although the most commonly investigated outcomes were psychological distress (N=22)and quality of life (N=16). The majority of studies relied on self-report measures, with only one study employing physiological measures of stress and inflammation (Lengacher et al., 2012).

Analytic strategies and reporting of results varied greatly between studies, and several studies failed to report results most pertinent to understanding the effect of the intervention. In the RCTs and multi-armed OTs, we were specifically interested in the relevant *time x group* interaction effects or post-intervention comparisons controlling for pre-intervention baseline scores when relevant. Uncontrolled within-group comparisons from multi-armed studies do not address the question of whether the intervention was effective, and are therefore not reported in Table 1. One-armed OTs are, by the nature of their design, unable to investigate controlled effects, and the pre-post within-group changes are therefore reported for those studies. In addition, one study included two groups differentiated only by one non-CBT component according to our definition (i.e., clinician reports; Chih et al., 2012), and the overall effect of time was therefore the most appropriate result to report from this study. All reported results are specific to the ICs unless otherwise noted.

Fifty-one percent of the studies produced at least one positive outcome (N=20), whereas 33% did not detect any effect of the intervention (N=13), and 15% did not report any inferential statistics due to a small sample size or did not report the relevant analyses (N=6). When studies produced a positive result, they most often did so for only one or two of the investigated outcomed, and studies did not consistently impact the same target. In six studies (Clark et al., 2013; Cohen & Kuten, 2006; Meyers et al., 2011; Northouse et al., 2007; 2013), quality of life was improved. Four studies (Bevans et al., 2013; Birnie, Garland, & Carlson, 2010; Cameron, Shin, Williams, & Stewart, 2004; DuBenske et al., 2013) found evidence for improvements of general measures of distress and/or mood/affect, coping was improved in three studies (Manne, Babb, Pinover, Horwitz, & Ebbert, 2004; Northouse et al., 2007; 2013), and three studies reported improved IC self-efficacy (Bevans et al., 2013; Keefe et al., 2005; Northouse et al., 2013) following the intervention.

DISCUSSION

The 39 studies reviewed demonstrated great variation in treatment components used and outcomes investigated. Demographic characteristics, both within and between studies, showed little variation with the majority of studies treating white, female ICs. Regarding overall treatment effects, a little over half of the studies reviewed in this chapter produced at least one positive outcome. There were no consistent relationships between studies obtaining positive results and patient stage of disease, treatment components used, or study design. Ten studies used an active control group, possibly hindering the emergence of an incremental effect of CBT. Additionally, the duration of intervention and follow-up periods varied considerably between studies, and longer follow-up periods may have muted the effect of interventions with less durable effects. While none of the three telephone-based interventions produced positive results (Budin et al., 2008; Campbell et al., 2007; Porter et al., 2011), this number of interventions is too small to draw a general conclusion about their capacity to deliver an effective CBT. Moreover, many studies reported a large number of comparisons, finding positive results on subscales only, which could simply be due to chance. Moreover, several studies failed to find, or did not report results in terms of the *time x group* interaction effect, and/or only found differences at one time point.

The most commonly used technique in the reviewed studies was reframing or restructuring. In traditional CBT, these techniques are used to challenge the content of negative thoughts, for instance by investigating the evidence for and against a belief (Clark & Beck, 2010). Such techniques are based on the more or less explicit assumption that there are cognitive errors to be corrected, and that a change of thought content will produce the desired emotional change. However, in the setting of psycho-oncology, there is often validity to potentially distorted or negative thoughts, and traditional cognitive restructuring approaches may therefore be experienced by the patient as invalidating (e.g., a patient who states "I am scared my husband will die" may, indeed, face the loss of her husband; Levin & Applebaum, in press).

The majority of studies focused mainly on reducing the negative impact of caregiving. However, the mere absence or reduction of negative impact does not constitute true gains or rewards. While caregiver burden has been well-documented, the benefits of providing care have received less attention, and only two of the reviewed studies explicitly examined gains or potentially rewarding experiences associated with being an IC (Baucom et al., 2009; Manne, Babb, Pinover, Horwitz, & Ebbert, 2004). Yet, there is emerging evidence for the potential rewards of providing care, including gaining meaning in life, increased appreciation of others, improved family functioning, and lower mortality (e.g., Applebaum, Farran, Marziliano, Pasternak, & Breitbart, 2014; Brown, Nesse, Vinokur, & Smith, 2003; Green, Wells, & Laakso, 2011; Haley et al., 2003; Kang et al., 2013; Mosher, Bakas, & Champion, 2013). Together, this work suggests that perceived severity of the caregiving burden is not directly associated with diminished reward (e.g., Kang et al., 2013), and that ICs may simultaneously experience both negative and positive emotions (e.g., Folkman & Moskowitz, 2000; Manne et al., 2004;

Mosher et al., 2013). As such, it has been suggested that interventions should focus both on the reduction of negative impact and on the enhancement of the potential benefits of caregiving (Li & Loke, 2013; Mosher et al., 2013; Williams & Bakitas, 2012). Based on the present results, it remains unknown whether CBTs promote an experience of growth and reward.

With respect to methodology, a range in number and quality of outcome measures was observed. The large number of different outcome measures used may reflect a lack of consistency and agreement in the field concerning both what should constitute primary outcomes and how to best measure these concepts of interest. In line with this, Hudson and colleagues (2010) highlighted that many instruments used to evaluate caregiver burden have not been developed for and validated among caregivers, and that the psychometric properties in many cases are thus poor or unexplored. Furthermore, self-report measures were employed in all included studies, and only one study included physiological measures (i.e., cortisol and pro-inflammatory markers; Lengagher et al., 2012).

A large proportion of the reviewed studies reported relatively high attrition, with no clear commonalities between studies with high attrition. This may be due to caregivers receiving sufficient support outside the formal psychotherapeutic arena, in addition to their well-documented struggle to prioritize their own self-care.

Worry and Rumination: Mechanisms of Distress

In terms of psychological burden of ICs, the chief complaint identified is often described as distress (e.g., Askari et al., 2012; Hudson et al., 2011; McLean et al., 2011; Mellon et al., 2006), which presents as anxious and depressive symptomatology. Distress is, however, not limited to anxiety and depressive symptoms, but is an emotional response that may manifest itself in a variety of ways, including poor sleep, poor self-efficacy, and marital dissatisfaction. It is noteworthy that the most investigated outcome was distress, yet, most interventions failed to impact this particular outcome.

Recent advances in the basic affective sciences stress that emotional responses have developed for the purpose of gaining security or reward, and our actions are guided by the motivational salience of the stimuli we encounter (Gray & McNaughton, 2000; Lang, 1995). Motivational conflicts may arise when both the security and reward systems are activated. Such conflicts are emotionally evocative, and the individual's ability to resolve these conflicts, in part, relies on the adaptive regulation of associated emotions (Mennin, Ellard, Fresco, & Gross, 2013; Stein & Paulus, 2009). A variety of motivational conflicts may arise as a result of taking responsibility for the care of a patient with cancer. A prominent conflict for ICs is balancing self-care and care for the patient, in which the IC may feel the need to leave the house or the hospital and at the same time experience fear and guilt in thinking about leaving the patient. The IC may also wish to have positive experiences with the patient while concurrently feeling distress about the anticipated loss of their loved one. Similarly, ICs may fear the death of their loved one but also imagine an easier future post bereavement.

Worry and rumination are common cognitive reactions to motivational conflicts (Borkovec & Sharpless, 2004; Mennin & Fresco, 2013), and involve repetitive thinking about future threats and past losses, respectively. These processes are self-referential, verbally mediated, cognitively elaborate, and have been conceptualized as maladaptive emotion regulation (e.g., Etkin & Schatzberg, 2011; Joormann, Dkane, & Gotlib, 2006, Mennin & Fresco, 2013). Emotion regulation, in this case, refers to what an individual does attentionally, meta-cognitively, and behaviorally in a given emotionally evocative moment, and has been distinguished from *coping* that typically concerns affective coping over much longer periods of time (e.g., coping with bereavement; Gross & Thompson, 2007). ICs have been found to engage in *worry,* e.g., thoughts about future trauma and loss, as well as *rumination,* e.g., thought concerning reasons for the cancer onset (Carmack Taylor et al., 2008; Gaugler, Eppinger, King, Sandberg, & Regine, 2013; Mosher, Jaynes, Hanna, & Ostroff, 2013; Rivera, 2009; Walker & Pomeroy, 1996). These processes have been shown to account for a large portion of the overall distress experienced by ICs (e.g., Carmack Taylor et al., 2008; Gaugler et al., 2013). It is noteworthy that none of the reviewed studies specifically targeted worry and/or rumination, although they may have done so implicitly through the various cognitive intervention components used, such as challenging the content of thoughts through restructuring techniques or gaining a decentered perspective through mindfulness-based techniques.

Proposed Target Mechanisms in CBT for ICs

Given the lack of consistent impact on caregiver burden and associated distress by previous CBT interventions, possible avenues for future CBTs should be highlighted. We propose that future interventions aim to directly target the very mechanisms through which distress may emerge (cf. Mennin et al., 2013). One such mechanism is emotion regulation. Improved emotion regulation skills may increase an individual's awareness of motivational conflicts and increase the likelihood that they respond to these conflicts in more adaptive ways. An example of such a therapy is Emotion Regulation Therapy (ERT), which directly targets emotion regulation (Mennin & Fresco, 2014). ERT is a contemporary, emotion-focused CBT that specifically targets emotional responses and underlying motivations. Organized around *three core target mechanisms*, ERT seeks to (1) increase motivational awareness, (2) develop emotion regulatory capacities, and (3) engage new contextual learning repertoires. ERT integrates traditional cognitive-behavioral approaches with basic and translational findings in affect science and promotes a balanced, proactive stance to emotional and environmental challenges (O'Toole, Mennin, & Fresco, 2014).

To date, ERT has shown promising results in treating anxiety and depression. A recently concluded NIMH-funded OT (N = 19; Mennin, Fresco, Heimberg, & Ritter, under review) and a RCT (N = 60; Mennin & Fresco, 2011; Mennin, Fresco, Heimberg, & Cieasla, 2012) have shown positive effects of ERT for individuals suffering from chronic anxiety and depression. In terms of clinical outcomes, both RCT and OT participants evidenced reductions in clinician-assessed and self-report measures of worry, trait anxious, and depression symptoms, and corresponding improvements in quality of life (Cohen's d = 1.5 to 4.5).

CONCLUSION AND LIMITATIONS

In comparison to other intervention types, interventions containing CBT components have been proposed to produce the largest effects for ICs (Applebaum & Breitbart, 2012; Sörensen et al., 2002). We therefore narratively reviewed the currently available 39 CBT intervention studies for ICs. Most studies were RCTs investigating CBT characterized by reframing techniques. We have argued that such techniques should be used with caution in the IC population, wherein the validity of negative thoughts/beliefs can be high. The majority of studies focused on reducing the negative impact of being an IC, and only two studies explicitly focused on the ability of CBT to promote growth and reward. Regarding attrition, rates varied greatly between studies, but were in general rather high, possibly reflecting ICs' motivational conflict of providing care for others versus self.

A little over half of the studies reported at least one positive outcome, and one may thus conclude that ICs are likely to experience some psychological improvement following CBT. However, several studies failed to find a positive effect, but no clear commonalities were detected between the studies that did or did not find an effect. Furthermore, many studies failed to report results from appropriate statistical analyses and only found differences at one time point or on one of many investigated subscales/outcomes. These issues are crucial when interpreting the results from the present review. Finally, the generalizability of the findings is limited due to the inclusion of participants who were primarily white, middle-aged, American women whose husbands or partners were diagnosed with cancer.

The purpose of the present review was first and foremost to provide a description of characteristics and targets of existing CBTs for ICs. Secondarily, we provided a narrative description of the effects of the interventions. To establish the magnitude and precision of the effects, meta-analytic efforts are necessary, and future studies should look further into determining the overall effect of CBT. The present review has highlighted the descriptive characteristics of the available research and provided the framework for such efforts. Given the relatively limited effects found of CBT for ICs, we have proposed an emotion regulation framework for understanding the distress experienced by ICs to guide the development of more effective interventions. We plan to investigate the effect of ERT for ICs, which directly targets the mechanisms through which distress is thought to emerge and be sustained. Furthermore, the ERT model is in accordance with the growing focus in the fields of psychooncology and palliative care on benefit finding and the potentially rewarding aspects of providing care.

REFERENCES

Akechi, T., Akizuki, N., Okamura, M., Shimizu, K., Oba, A., Ito, T. ... Uchitomi, Y. (2006). Psychological distress experienced by families of cancer patients: Preliminary findings from psychiatric consultation of a cancer center hospital. *Japanese Journal of Clinical Oncology, 36*, 329-332.

Applebaum, A. J., & Breitbart, W. (2013). Care for the cancer caregiver: A systematic review. *Palliative Supportive Care, 11*, 231-252.

Applebaum, A. J., Farran, C. J., Marziliano, A. M., Pasternak, A. R., & Breitbart, W. (2014). Preliminary study of themes of meaning and psychosocial service use among informal cancer caregivers. *Palliative Supportive Care, 12,* 139-148.

Askari, A., Madgaonkar, S. J., & Rowell, R. K. (2012). Current psychopathological issues among partners of cancer patients. *Journal of Psychosocial Research, 7,* 77-85.

Baider, L., & Kaplan De-Nour, A. (1988). Adjustment to cancer: Who is the patient—the husband or the wife? *Israel Journal of Medicine and Science, 24,* 631–636.

Baider, L., Kaufman, B., Perez, T., Manor, O., Everhadani, P., & Kaplan De-Nour, A. (1996). Mutuality of fate: Adaptation and psychological distress in cancer patients and their partners. In L. Baider, C. L. Cooper, & A. K. De-Nour (Eds.), *Cancer and the family* (pp. 173–186). New York: Wiley.

Baucom, D. H., Porter, L. S., Kirby, J. S., Gremore, T. M., Wiesenthal, N., Aldrige, W. ... Keefe, F. J. (2009). A couple-based intervention for female breast cancer. *Psycho-Oncology, 18*, 276–283.

Bevans, M., Castro, K., Prince, P., Shelburne, N., Prachenko, O., Loscalzo, M. ... Zabora, J. (2010). An individualized dyadic problem-solving education intervention for patients and family caregivers during allogeneic HSCT: A feasibility study. *Cancer Nursing, 33,* E24–E32.

Bevans, M., Wehrlen, L., Castro, K., Prince, P., Shelburne, N., Soeken, K. ... Wallen, G. R. (2014). A problem-solving education intervention in caregivers and patients during allogeneic hematopoietic stem cell transplantation. *Journal of Health Psychology, 19,* 602-617.

Birnie, K., Garland, S. N., & Carlson, L. E. (2010). Psychological benefits for cancer patients and their partners participating in mindfulness-based stress reduction (MBSR). *Psycho-Oncology, 19*, 1004-1009.

Blanchard, C. G., Toseland, R. W., & McCallion, P. (1996). The effects of a problem-solving intervention with spouses of cancer patients. *Journal of Psychosocial Oncology, 14*, 11–21.

Borkovec, T., & Sharpless, B. (2004). Generalized anxiety disorder: Bringing cognitive behavioral therapy into the valued present. In S. C. Hayes, V. Follette, & M. Linehan (Eds.), *Mindfulness and Acceptance: Expanding the cognitive-behavioral traditional*. New York: The Guilford Press.

Braun, M., Mikulincer, M., Rydall, A., Walsh, A., & Rodin, G. (2007). Hidden morbidity in cancer: Spouse caregivers. *Journal of Clinical Oncology, 25*, 4829-4834.

Brown, S. L., Nesse, R. M., Vinokur, A. D., & Smith, D. M. (2003). Providing social support may be more beneficial than receiving it: Results from a prospective study of mortality. *Psychological Science, 14*, 320-327.

Budin, W. C., Hoskins, C. N., Haber, J., Sherman, D. W., Maislin, G., Carter, J. R. ... Shukla, S. (2008). Breast cancer: Education, counseling and adjustment among patients and partners: A randomized clinical trial. *Nursing Research, 57*, 199–213.

Burton, L. C., Newsom, J. T., Schulz, R., Hirsch, C. H., German, P. S. (1997). Preventive health behaviors among spousal caregivers. *Preventive Medicine, 26,* 162–169.

Butow, P. N., Price, M. A., Bell, M. L., Webb, P. M., deFazio, A., & Friedlander, M. (2014). Caring for women with ovarian cancer in the last year of life: A longitudinal study of caregiver quality of life, distress and unmet needs. *Gynecologic Oncology, 132*, 690-697.

Cameron, J. I., Shin, J. L., Williams, D., & Stewart, D. E. (2004). A brief problem-solving intervention for family caregivers to individuals with advanced cancer. *Journal of Psychosomatic Research, 57*, 137-143.

Campbell, L. C., Keefe, F. J., Scipio, C., McKee, D. C., Edwards, C. L., Herman, S. H. ... Donatucci, C. (2007). Facilitating research participation and improving quality of life for African American prostate cancer survivors and their intimate partners: A pilot study of telephone-based coping skills training. *Cancer, 109,* S414–S424.

Canada, A. L., Neese, L. E., Sui, D., & Schover, L. R. (2005). Pilot intervention to enhance sexual rehabilitation for couples after treatment for localized prostate carcinoma. *Cancer, 104,* 2689-2700.

Carmack Taylor, C. L., Badr, H., Lee, J. H., Fossella, F., Pisters, K., Gritz, E. R., & Schover, L. (2008). Lung cancer patients and their spouses: Psychological and relationship functioning within 1 month of treatment initiation. *Annals of Behavior Medicine, 36*, 129-140.

Carter, P. A. (2003). Family caregivers' sleep loss and depression over time. *Cancer Nursing, 26*, 253-259.

Carter, P. A. (2006). A brief behavioral sleep intervention for family caregivers of persons with cancer. *Cancer Nursing, 29,* 95–103.

Chih, M., DuBenske, L. L., Hawkins, R. P., Brown, R. L., Dinauer, S. K., Cleary, J. F., & Gustafson, D. H., (2012). Communicating advanced cancer patients' symptoms via the internet: A pooled analysis of two randomized trials examining caregiver preparedness, physical burden, and negative mood. *Palliative Medicine, 27*, 533-543.

Cho, M. H., Dodd, M. J., Lee, K. A., Padilla, G., & Slaughter, R. (2006). Self-reported sleep quality in family caregivers of gastric cancer patients who are receiving chemotherapy in Korea. *Journal of Cancer Education: The*

Official Journal of the American Association for Cancer Education, 21(1 Suppl), S37-S41.

Christakis, N. A., & Allison, P. D. (2006). Mortality after the hospitalization of a spouse. *New England Journal of Medicine, 354,* 719–730.

Christensen, D. N. (1983). Postmastectomy couple counseling: An outcome study of a structured treatment protocol. *Journal of Sex and Marital Therapy, 9,* 266–275.

Clark, D. A., & Beck, A. T. (2010). *Cognitive therapy of anxiety disorders. Science and practice.* New York: The Guilford Press.

Clark., M. M., Rummans, T. A., Artherton, P. J., Cheville, A. L., Johnson, M. E., Frost, M. H. ... Brown, P. D. (2013). Randomized controlled trial of maintaining quality of life during radiotherapy for advanced cancer. *Cancer, 119*, 880-887.

Clark, M. M., Rummans, T. A., Sloan, J. A., Jensen, A., Atherton, P. J., Frost, M. H. ... Brown, P. D. (2006). Quality of life of caregivers of patients with advanced-stage cancer. *American Journal of Hospice & Palliative Medicine, 23*, 185-191.

Clavarino, A. M., Lowe, J. B., Carmont, S. A., & Barlanda, K. (2002). The needs of cancer patients and their families from rural and remote areas of Queensland. *Australian Journal of Rural Health, 10*, 188-195.

Cliff, A. M., & MacDonagh, R. P. (2000). Psychosocial morbidity in prostate cancer: II. A comparison of patients and partners. *British Journal of Urology International, 86*, 834-839.

Cohen, M., & Kuten, A. (2006). Cognitive-behavior group intervention for relatives of cancer patients: A controlled study. *Journal of Psychosomatic Research, 61,* 187–196.

DuBenske, L. L., Gustafson, D. H., Namkoong, K., Hawkins, R. P., Atwood, A. K., Brown, R. ... Cleary, J. F. (2013, November 18). CHESS Improves Cancer Caregivers' Burden and Mood: Results of an eHealth RCT . *Health Psychology*. Advance online publication.

Etkin, A., & Schatzberg, A. F. (2011). Common abnormalities and disorder-specific compensation during implicit regulation of emotional processing in generalized anxiety and major depressive disorders. *American Journal of Psychiatry, 168*, 968–978.

Fegg, M. J., Brandstättir, M., Kögler, M., Hauke, G., Rechenberg-Winter, P., Fensterer, V. ... Borasio, G. D. (2013). Existential behavioural therapy for informal caregivers of palliative patients: a randomised controlled trial. *Psycho-Oncology, 22*, 2079-2086.

Ferrario, S. R., Zotti, A. M., Massara, G., & Nuvolone, G. (2003). A comparative assessment of psychological and psychosocial characteristics of cancer patients and their caregivers. *Psycho-Oncology, 12*, 1-7.

Folkman, S., & Moskowitz, J. T. (2000). Positive affect and the other side of coping. *American Psychologist*, 55, 647-654.

Gallagher, J., Parle, M., & Cairns, D. (2002). Appraisal and psychological distress six months after diagnosis of breast cancer. *British Journal of Health Psychology, 7*, 365-376.

Gaugler, J. E., Eppinger, A., King, J., Sandberg, T., & Regine, W. F. (2013). Coping and its effect on cancer caregiving. *Supportive Care in Cancer, 21*, 385-395.

Girgis, A., Lambert, S. D., McElduff, P., Bonevski, B., Lecathelinais, C., Boyes, A., & Stacey, F. (2013). Some things change, some things stay the same: A longitudinal analysis of cancer caregivers' unmet supportive care needs. *Psycho-Oncology, 22*, 1557-1564.

Given, B., & Given, C.W. (1992). Patient and family caregiver reaction to new and recurrent breast cancer. *Journal of the American Medical Women's Association, 47,* 201–206.

Given, B., Given, C. W., Sikorskii, A., Jeon, S., Sherwood, P., & Rahbar, M. (2006). The impact of providing symptom management assistance on caregiver reaction: Results of a randomized trial. *Journal of Pain and Symptom Management, 32,* 433–443.

Given, C.W., Stommel, M., Given, B.A., Osuch, J., Kurtz, M. E, & Kurtz, J. C. (1993). The influence of cancer patients' symptoms and functional status on patients' depression and family caregivers' reaction and depression. *Health Psychology, 12,* 277–285.

Given, B., Wyatt, G., Given, C., Sherwood, P., Gift, A., DeVosss, D., & Rahbar, M (2004). Burden and depression among caregivers of patients with cancer at the end of life. *Oncology Nursing Forum, 31,* 1105–1117.

Gray, J. A., & McNaughton, N. (2000) *The neuropsychology of anxiety: An Enquiry into the functions of the septo-hippocampal system* (2nd ed.). (Oxford Psychology Series No. 33). Oxford: Oxford University Press.

Green, H. J., Wells, D. J., & Laakso, L. (2011). Coping in men with prostate cancer and their partners: A quantitative and qualitative study. *European Journal of Cancer Care, 20*, 237-247.

Gross, J. J., & Thompson, R. A. (2007). Emotion Regulation: Conceptual Foundations. In J. J. Gross (Ed.), *Handbook of Emotion Regulation* (1st ed.) (pp. 3–24). New York: The Guilford Press.

Haley, W. E., LaMonde, L. A., Han, B., Burton, A. M., & Schonweitter, R. (2003). Predictors of depression and life satisfaction among spousal caregivers in hospice: Application of a stress process model. *Journal of Palliative Medicine, 6,* 215-224.

Harden, J., Falahee, M., Bickes, J., Schafenacker, A., Walker, J., Mood, D., & Northouse, L. (2009). Factors associated with prostate cancer patients' and their spouses' satisfaction with a family-based intervention. *Cancer Nursing, 32*, 482-492.

Hearson, B., & McClement, S. (2007). Sleep disturbance in family caregivers of patients with advanced cancer. *International Journal of Palliative Nursing, 13*, 495-501.

Heinrich, R. L., & Schag, C. C. (1985). Stress and activity management: Group treatment for cancer patients and spouses. *Journal of Consulting and Clinical Psychology, 53,* 439–446.

Hofmann, S. G., Asnaani, A., Vonk, I. J. J., Sawyer, A. T., & Fang, A. (2012). The efficacy of cognitive behavioral therapy: A review of meta-analyses. *Cognitive Therapy and Research, 36*, 427-440.

Hofmann, S. G., & Smits, J. A. (2008). Cognitive-behavioral therapy for adult anxiety disorders: A meta-analysis of randomized placebo-controlled trials. *Journal of Clinical Psychiatry, 69*, 621-632.

Hudson, P., & Payne, S. (2009). The future of family caregiving: Research, social policy and clinical practice. In P. Hudson, & S. Payne (Eds.), *Family carers in palliative care: A guide for health and social care professionals* (pp. 277-303). Oxford: Oxford University Press.

Hudson, P. L., Thomas, K., Trauer, T., Remedios, C., & Clarke, D. (2011). Psychological and social profile of family caregivers on commencement of palliative care. *Journal of Pain and Symptom Management, 41*, 522-534.

Hudson, P. L., Trauer, T., Graham, S., Grande, G., Ewing, G., Payne, S. ...Thomas, K. (2010). A systematic review of instruments related to family caregivers of palliative care patients. *Palliative Medicine, 24*, 656-668.

Janda, M., Steginga, S., Dunn, J., Langbecker, D., Walker, D., Eakin, E. (2008). Unmet supportive needs and interest in services among patients with a brain tumor and their carers. *Patient Education and Counseling, 71*, 251-258.

Jemal, A., Bray, F., Center, M. M., Ferley, J., Ward, E., & Forman, D. (2011). Global cancer statistics. *CA: A Cancer Journal for Clinicians, 61*, 69-90.

Jensen, S., & Given, B. A. (1991). Fatigue affecting family caregivers of cancer patients. *Cancer Nursing, 14*, 181-187.

Joormann, J., Dkane, M., & Gotlib, I. H. (2006). Adaptive and maladaptive components of rumination? Diagnostic specificity and relation to depressive biases. *Behavior Therapy, 37*, 269-280.

Kang, J., Shin, D. W., Choi, J. E., Sanjo, M., Yoon, S. J., Kim, H. K. ... Yoon, W. H. (2013). Factors associated with positive consequences of serving as a family caregiver for a terminal cancer patient. *Psycho-Oncology, 22*, 564-571.

Kayser, K., Feldman, B. N., Borstelmann, N. A., & Daniels, A. A. (2010). Effects of a randomized couple-based intervention on quality of life of breast cancer patients and their partners. *Social Work Research, 34*, 20-32.

Keefe, F., Ahles, T., Sutton, L., Dalton, J., Baucom, D., Pope, M. S. ... Scipio, C. (2005). Partner-guided cancer pain management at the end of life: A preliminary study. *Journal of Pain and Symptom Management, 29,* 263–272.

Kiecolt-Glaser, J.K., Glaser, R., Shuttleworth, E.C., Dyer, C. S., Ogrocki, P. & Speicher, C. E. (1987). Chronic stress and immunity in family caregivers of Alzheimer's disease victims. *Psychosomatic Medicine, 49*, 523–535.

Kim, Y., Shaffer, K. M., Carver, C. S., & Cannady, R. S. (2014). Prevalence and predictors of depressive symptoms among cancer caregivers 5 years after the relative's cancer diagnosis. *Journal of Consulting and Clinical Psychology, 82*, 1-8.

Kögler, M., Brandstätter, M., Borasio, G. D., Fensterer, V., Küchenhoff, H., & Fegg, M. J. (2013, June 17). Mindfulness in informal caregiver of palliative patients. *Palliative Supportive Care.* E-pub ahead of print.

Kornblith, A. B., Herr, H. W., Ofman, U. S., Scher, H. I., & Hollands, J. C. (1994). Quality of life of patients with prostate cancer and their spouses. the value of a data base in clinical care. *Cancer, 73*, 2791-2802.

Kris, A. E., Cherlin, E. J., Prigerson, H., Carlson, M. D., Johnson-Hurzeler, R., Kasl, S. V., & Bradley, E. H. (2006). Length of hospice enrollment and subsequent depression in family caregivers: 13-month follow-up study. *American Geriatric Psychiatry, 14*, 264-269.

Kuijer, R.G., Buunk, B.P., De Jong, G.M., Ybema, j. F., & Sanderman, R. (2004). Effects of a brief intervention program for patients with cancer and their partners on feelings of inequity, relationship quality, and psychological distress. *Psycho-Oncology, 13,* 321–334.

Kurtz, M.E., Kurtz, J.C., Given, C.W., & Given, B. A. (2005). Depression and physical health among family caregivers of geriatric patients with cancer - a longitudinal view. *Medical Science Monitor, 10*, CR447–456.

Lambert, S. D., Gigis, A., Lecathelinais, C., & Stacey, F. (2013). Walking a mile in their shoes: Anxiety and depression among partners and caregivers of cancer survivors at 6 and 12 months post-diagnosis. *Supportive Cancer Care, 21,* 75-85.

Lambert, S. D., Jones, B. L., Gigis, A., & Lecathelinais, C. (2012). Distressed partners and caregivers do not recover easily: Adjustment trajectories among partners and caregivers of cancer survivors. *Annals of Behavioral Medicine, 44*, 225-235.

Lang, P. J. (1995). The emotion probe: Studies of motivation and attention. *American Psychologist, 50*, 372-385.

Lee, S., Colditz, G. A., Berkman, L. F., & Kawachi, I. (2003). Caregiving and risk of coronary heart disease in U.S. women: A prospective study. *American Journal of Preventive Medicine, 24*, 113–119.

Lengacher, C. A., Kip, K. E., Barta, M., Post-White, J., Jacobsen, P. B., Groer, M. ... Shelton, M. M. (2012). A pilot study evaluating the effect of mindfulness-based stress reduction on psychological status, physical status, salivary cortisol, and interleukin-6 among advanced-stage cancer patients and their caregivers. *Journal of Holistic Nursing: Official Journal of the American Holistic Nurses' Association, 30*, 170-185.

Levin, T., & Applebaum, A. (in press). Acute cancer cognitive therapy. *Cognitive and Behavioral Practice.*

Li, Q., & Loke, A. Y. (2013). The positive aspects of caregiving for cancer patients: A critical review of the literature and directions for future research. *Psycho-Oncology, 22*, 2399-2407.

Manne, S., Babb, J., Pinover, W., Horwitz, E., & Ebbert, J. (2004). Psychoeducational group intervention for wives of men with prostate cancer. *Psycho-Oncology, 13,* 37–46.

Manne, S. L., Kissane, D. W., Nelson, C. J., Mulhall, J. P., Winkel, G., & Zaider, T. (2011). Intimacy-enhancing psychological intervention for men diagnosed with prostate cancer and their partners: A pilot study. *Journal of Sexual Medicine, 8*, 1197-1209.

Mazanec, S. R., Daly, B. J., Douglas, S. L., & Lipson, A. R. (2011). Work productivity and health of informal caregivers of persons with advanced cancer. *Research in Nursing & Health, 34*, 483-495.

McLean, L. M., Walton, T., Matthew, A., & Jones, J. M. (2011). Examination of couples ' attachment security in relation to depression and hopelessness in maritally distressed patients facing end-stage cancer and their spouse caregivers: A buffer or facilitator of psychosocial distress? *Supportive Care in Cancer: Official Journal of the Multinational Association of Supportive Care in Cancer, 19,* 1539-1548.

McMillan, S. C., Small, B. J., Weitzner, M., Schonwetter, R., Tittle, M., Moody, L., & Haley, W. E. (2005). Impact of coping skills intervention with family caregivers of hospice patients with cancer. *Cancer, 106,* 214–222.

Mellon, S., Northouse, L. L., & Weiss, L. K. (2006). A population-based study of the quality of life of cancer survivors and their family caregivers. *Cancer Nursing, 29*, 120-131.

Mennin, D. S., & Fresco, D. M. (2011, November). Emotion Regulation Therapy for complex and refractory presentations of anxiety and depression. A spotlight presentation delivered at the annual meeting of the Association for Behavioral and Cognitive Therapies, Toronto, Ontario.

Mennin, D. S. & Fresco, D. M. (2013). What, me worry and ruminate about DSM-5 and RDoC?: The importance of targeting negative self-referential processing. *Clinical Psychology: Science and Practice, 20,* 259-268.

Mennin, D. S., Ellard, K. K., Fresco, D. M., & Gross, J. J. (2013). United we stand: Emphasizing commonalities of cognitive-behavioral therapies. *Behavior Therapy, 44,* 234-248.

Mennin, D. S., & Fresco, D. M. (2014). Emotion Regulation Therapy. In J. J.Gross, *Handbook of emotion regulation* (2nd ed.) (pp.469-490). New York: The Guilford Press.

Mennin, D. S., Fresco, D. M., Heimberg, R. G., & Ciesla, J. (2012, April). Randomized control trial of Emotion Regulation Therapy for generalized anxiety disorder and comorbid depression. In M. Fraire & T. Ollendick (Chairs), Emotion Regulation in Anxiety Disorders Across the Lifespan: Comorbidity & Treatment. Paper presented at the annual meeting of the Anxiety Disorders Association of America, Arlington, VA.

Mennin, D. S., Fresco, D.M., Heimberg, R.G., & Ritter, M. *An open trial of emotion regulation therapy for generalized anxiety disorder and comorbid depression.* Manuscript under review.

Meyers, F. J., Carducci, M., Loscalzo, M. J., Linder, J., Greasby, T., & Beckett, L. A. (2011). Effects of problem-solving intervention (COPE) on quality of life for patients with advanced cancer on clinical trials and their caregivers: Simultaneous care and educational intervention (SCEI): Linking palliation and clinical trials. *Journal of Palliative Medicine, 14,* 465-473.

Mosher, C. E., Bakas, T., & Champion, V. L. (2013). Physical health, mental health, and life changes among family caregivers of patients with lung cancer. *Oncology Nursing Forum, 40*, 53-61.

Mosher, C. E., Jaynes, H. A., Hanna, N., & Ostroff, J. S. (2013). Distressed family caregivers of lung cancer patients: An examinatino of psychosocial and practical challenges. *Supportive Care in Cancer, 21*, 431-437.

Muraven, M.R., & Baumeister, R.F. (2000). Self-regulation and depletion of limited resources: Does self-control resemble a muscle? *Psychological Bulletin, 126*, 247-259.

National Alliance for Caregiving in Collaboration with, AARP. (2009). *Caregiving in the U.S.* Retrieved from http://www.caregiving.org/data/CaregivingUSAllAgesExec-Sum.pdf.

Nenova, M., Morris, L., Paul, L, Yuelin, L., Applebaum, A., & DuHamel, K. (2013). Psychosocial interventions with cognitive-behavioral components for the treatment of cancer-related traumatic stress symptoms: A review of randomized controlled trials. *Journal of Cognitive Psychotherapy, 27*, 258-284.

Newman, M. G., Przeworski, A., Fisher, A. J., & Borkovec, T. D. (2010). Diagnostic comorbidity in adults with generalized anxiety disorder: Impact of comorbidity on psychotherapy outcome and impact of psychotherapy on comorbid diagnoses. *Behavior Therapy, 41,* 59-72.

Northouse, L. L., Katapodi, M. C., Song, L., Zhang, L., & Mood, D. W. (2010). Interventions with family caregivers of cancer patients: Meta-analysis of randomized trials. *CA: A Cancer Journal for Clinicians, 60*, 317-339.

Northouse, L., Kershaw, T., Mood, D., & Schafenacker, A. (2005). Effects of a family intervention on the quality of life of women with recurrent breast cancer and their family caregivers. *Psycho-Oncology, 14*, 478–491.

Northouse, L. L., Mood, D. W., Schafenacker, A., Kalemkerian, G., Zalupski, M., LoRusso, P. ... Kershaw, T. (2013). Randomized clinical trial of a brief and extensive dyadic intervention for advanced cancer patients and their family caregivers. *Psycho-Oncology, 22*, 555-563.

Northouse, L. L., Mood, D. W., Schafenacker, A., Montie, J. E., Sandler, H. M., Forman, J. D. ... Kershew, T. (2007). Randomized clinical trial of a family intervention for prostate cancer patients and their spouses. *Cancer, 110*, 2809-2818.

O'Toole, M. S., Mennin, D. S., & Fresco, D. M. (in press). Emotion Regulation Therapy: An experiential approach to chronic anxiety and recurring depression. In: N. C. Thoma, & D. McKay (eds.). Working with emotion in cognitive-behavioral therapy: Techniques for clinical practice. New York: The Guilford Press.

Pariante, C. M., Carpiniello, B., Orru, M. G., Sitzia, R., Piras, A., Farci, A. M., Del Giacco, G. S., Piludu, G., & Miller, A. H. (1997). Chronic caregiving stress alters peripheral blood immune parameters: The role of age and severity of stress. *Journal of Psychotherapy and Psychosomatics, 66*, 199–207.

Porter, L. S., Keefe, F. J., Baucom, D. H., Hurwitz, H., Moser, B., Patternson, E., & Kim, H. J. (2009). Partner-assisted emotional disclosure for patients with gastrointestinal cancer. *Cancer, 115(18 suppl)*, 4326-4338.

Porter, L. S., Keefe, F. J., Garst, J., Baucom, D. H., McBride, C. M. McKee, D. C. ... Scipio, C. (2011). Caregiver-assisted coping skills training for lung cancer: Results of a randomized clinical trial. *Journal of Pain and Symptom Management, 41,* 1-13.

Reele, B. L. (1994). Effect of counseling on quality of life for individuals with cancer and their families. *Cancer Nursing, 17*, 101–112.

Rivera, H. R. (2009). Depression symptoms in cancer caregivers. *Clinical Journal of Oncology Nursing, 13*, 195-202.

Rohleder, N., Marin, T.J., Ma, R., & Miller, G. E. (2009). Biologic cost of caring for a cancer patient: Dysregulation of pro and anti-inflammatory signaling pathways. *Journal of Clinical Oncology, 27*, 2909–2915.

Romito, F., Goldzweig, G., Cormio, C., Hagedoorn, M., & Andersen, B. L. (2013). Informal caregiving for cancer patients. *Cancer (11 supplement), 119*, 2160-2169.

Scanlan, J. M., Vitaliano, P. P., Zhang, J., Savage, M., & Ochs, H. D. (2001). Lymphocyte proliferation is associated with gender, caregiving, and psychosocial variables in older adults. *Journal of Behavioral Medicine, 24,* 537-559.

Schover, L. R., Canada, A. L., Yuan, Y., Sui, D., Neese, L., Jenkins, R., & Rhodes, M. M. (2012). A randomized trial of internet-based versus traditional sexual counseling for couples after localized prostate cancer treatment. *Cancer, 118*, 500-509.

Schulz, R., & Beach, S.R. (1999). Caregiving as a risk factor for mortality: The caregiver health effects study. *Journal of the American Medical Association, 282,* 2215–2219.

Scott, K., & Beatty, L. (2013). Feasibility study of a self-guided cognitive behaviour therapy internet intervention for cancer carers. *Australian Journal of Primary Health, 19*, 270-274.

Scott, J. L., Halford, W.K. & Ward, B. (2004). United we stand? The effects of a couple-coping intervention on adjustment to early stage breast or gynecological cancer. *Journal of Consulting and Clinical Psychology, 72*, 1122–1135.

Siegel, R., DeSantis, C., Virgo, K., Stein, K., Meriotto, A., Smith, T. … Ward, E. (2012). Cancer treatment and survivorship statistics. *CA: A Cancer Journal for Clinicians, 62*, 220-241.

Sörensen, S., Pinquart, M. & Duberstein, P. (2002). How effective are interventions with caregivers? An updated meta-analysis. *The Gerontologist, 42,* 356–372.

Stein, M. B., & Paulus, M. P. (2009). Imbalance of Approach and Avoidance: The Yin and Yang of Anxiety Disorders. *Biological Psychiatry, 66*, 1072–1074.

Stenberg, U., Rulan, C. M., Miaskowski, C. (2010). Review of the literature on the effects of caring for a patient with cancer. *Psychooncology, 19,* 1013-1025.

Teel, C. S. Press, A. N., Lindgren, C. L., & Nichols, E. G. (1999). Fatigue among elders in caregiving and noncaregiving roles. *Western Journal of Nursing Research, 21,* 498–520.

Toseland, R.W., Blanchard, C.G. & McCallion, P. (1995). A problem solving intervention for caregivers of cancer patients. *Social Science and Medicine, 40,* 517–528.

Vanderwerker, L. C., Laff, R. E., Kadan-Lottick, N. S., McColl, S., & Prigerson, H. G. (2005). Psychiatric disorders and mental health service use among caregivers of advanced cancer patients. *Journal of Clinical Oncology, 23*(28), 6899-6907.

Vitaliano, P. P., Scanlan, J. M., Ochs, H. D., Syrjala, K., Siegler, I. C., & Snyder, E. A. (1998). Psychosocial stress moderates the relationship of cancer history with natural killer cell activity. *Annals of Behavioral Medicine 20*, 199-208.

Vitaliano, P. P., Scanlan, J. M., Zhang, J., Savage, M. V., Hirsch, I. B., & Siegler, I. C. (2002). A path model of chronic stress, the metabolic syndrome, and coronary heart disease. *Psychosomatic Medicine, 64*, 418-435.

von Känel, R., Mausbach, B. T., Patterson, T. L., Dimsdale, J. E., Aschbacher, K., Mills, P. J. … Grant, I. (2008). Increased Framingham coronary heart disease risk score in dementia caregivers relative to non-caregiving controls. *Gerontology, 54,* 131–137.

Walker, R. J., & Pomeroy, E.C. (1996). Depression or grief? The experience of caregivers of people with dementia. *Health and Social Work, 21*, 247–254.

Williams, A. L., & Bakitas, M. (2012). Cancer family caregivers: A new direction for interventions. *Journal of Palliative Medicine, 15*, 775-783.

World Cancer Research Fund, International. *Cancer statistics*. Retrieved from http://www.wcrf.org/cancer_statistics/cancer_facts/index.php

Yobroff, K. R., & Kim, Y. (2009). Time costs associated with informal caregiving of cancer survivors. *Cancer, 115 (18 Suppl),* 4362-4373.

In: Cognitive Behavioral Therapy
Editor: Brendan Myers
ISBN: 978-1-63321-638-9

Chapter 4

COGNITIVE BEHAVIORAL THERAPY IN PAIN MANAGEMENT OF ADULT CHRONIC NONMALIGNANT PAIN PATIENTS*

***Jaroslava Raudenska*[1], *Jana Amlerova*[2] and *Alena Javurkova*[1,3]**

[1]Department of Clinical Psychology 2nd Faculty of Medicine, Charles University in Prague and Motol University Hospital, Prague, Czech Republic

[2]Department of Neurology 2nd Faculty of Medicine, Charles University in Prague and Motol University Hospital, Prague, Czech Republic

[3]Department of Clinical Psychology, Kralovske Vinohrady University Hospital, Prague, Czech Republic

ABSTRACT

The origin, course and subsequent maintenance of pain is influenced by psychosocial factors. For this reason, psychotherapy is also used in pain management and the use of cognitive behavioral therapy (CBT) is dominant. This chapter describes the history of CBT and its three basic approaches: behavioral, cognitive and cognitive-behavioral. The indication to CBT and the most frequent problems in treatment are

* Supported by Ministry of Health, Czech Republic - Conceptual Development of Research Organization, University Hospital Motol, Prague, Czech Republic 00064203.

defined. Basic CBT techniques in chronic pain management, namely cognitive restructuring and the practice of skills for pain and stress management (education, adaptive positive self-instruction, relaxation and imagination, graded activity, exposition, structured problem solving and relapse coping) are specified. Particular fields of chronic pain which represent the goal of the multidisciplinary program of pain management including CBT are examined. The authors structure the basic assumptions of a successful program: direct and indirect positive reinforcement of pain behavior, positive reinforcement of required behavior, improvement of physical condition, cognitive reframing, education, training in CBT in pain management and conforming to CBT principles. The chapter summarizes the efficiency of CBT in chronic non-malignant pain management in adult patients, describes problems in its monitoring and suggests some innovations increasing its use.

INTRODUCTION

Pain is a signal of threat to the body, or possibly life, and therefore represents a signal of the highest priority. At the time of its onset, pain interferes with central processes and influences attentional focus, constricts and reorganises mental and congnitive processes as well as behavior to the perceived threat and alters social communication processes in pain sufferers (Eccleston and Crombez, 1999). The feeling of pain and the cognitive appreciation of what pain means thus induce fear and, simultaneously, the processes of intensive mental coping with pain and related problems, so-called coping processes. These mechanisms are adaptive in acute pain, or with adequate cognitive appreciation of pain. If, however, the fear of pain, constricted attentional focus and catastrophic thinking persist to the same or slightly diminished degree in chronic pain, they are usually maladaptive. They deform and are more or less autonomous, almost independent of the current pathophysiological status. If these processes persist after the healing of the pain process, they are unambiguously pathological. Pain as a signal, however, may also be associated with loss of information, or a completely false signal (phantom pain, somatoform pain) may be concerned.

For basic classification, pain may be divided into malignant and nonmalignant pain, neuropathic and nociceptive pain, and mixed pain (representing most cases of chronic pain). Regarding the time factor, we divide pain into acute, chronic and recurrent. Chronic nonmalignant pain often persists beyond usual healing time, lacking the warning signal function. It is mostly caused by a combination of different factors such as injuries, disease and medical interventions. The psychologically complicated chronic pain state, however, is characterised by the fact that it often cannot be explained purely based on pathophysiology. A chronic pain patient experiences suffering, which is a cognitive-affective construct. It represents a loss of the sense of meaning, combined with depression. Specifically, it occurs in the third stage of psychological pain processing (Wade et al., 1996). This complex of generalized effects is relatively independent of the actual feeling of pain. The suffering may be a result of somatic, mental or social causes; thus it is a consequence of somatic, psychological or social processes. Chronic pain (duration and intensity) may lead to a more intensive feeling of jeopardy in the patient. This is associated with the anxiety-escape / anger-attack response, or with anxiety / anger / impossibility of escape/attack – i.e. with emotions (Spielberger et al., 2003). Emotions can influence the intensity of pain. This process involves unpleasantness and the neurophysiological aspects of the pain mechanism and analgesia (Price 1999; Price and Harkins 1992). Patients reporting a higher intensity of pain are more likely to experience depression, anxiety and anger than patients describing a lower intensity of pain. It is also often very difficult for a patient with chronic pain to deal with personal, social and relationship problems such as somatic restrictions, changes in life roles (as regards work, family or leisure) and legal problems due to pain. Patients with intensive chronic and persistent pain usually experience profound psychosocial distress as a consequence of long-lasting pain and only a small subjective effect of any treatment administered so far on their quality of life. For this reason, psychotherapy forms part of the multidisciplinary management of chronic nonmalignant pain.

BACKGROUND

In 1879, W. Wundt established the first psychology laboratory in Leipzig. Psychological approaches to pain management do not date back beyond this date. The term "psychogenic pain" was first used in 1904 by O. Binswanger. In 1909, E. Titchener founded a psychology lab in Cornell, USA, and observed that pain had not only sensory, but also emotional components. In 1920, I. P. Pavlov showed that a dog can have a conditioned response to a painful stimulus in a manner that is usually associated with being exposed to food. In 1965, R. Melzack and P. Wall published a paper on the gate theory of pain in which they provided a framework for understanding the relationship between a peripheral noxius stimulus and the experience of pain (Melzack and Wall,

1965). The theory showed that the transmission of pain messages may be modulated by somatic mechanisms as well as by non-specific modulation mechanisms (such as personal characteristics, mood, social impacts, learning, etc.) that can also decrease or increase the intensity of pain. In 1968, R. Melzack and K. Casey described the three basic dimensions of pain: 1. "sensory-discriminative" (intensity, location, quality and duration of the pain), 2. "affective-motivational" (unpleasantness of pain and urge to escape the unpleasantness) and 3. "cognitive-evaluative" (appraisal, cultural values, attentional distraction from pain and hypnotic suggestion) (Melzack and Casey, 1968). Their theory has shown that intensity (the sensory-discriminative dimension) and unpleasantness (the affective-motivational dimension) of pain are not influenced only by the volume and quantity of pain stimuli, but also by cognitive processes (the cognitive-evaluative dimension). Cognitive processes can influence both the sensory (intensity, quality) and affective experience (discomfort), or they primarily modify the affective-motivational dimension. That is why, for example, enthusiasm in a game, or excitement in a war, may block the 1st and 3rd dimension of pain, while suggestion and placebo may modulate the affective-motivational dimension and, at the same time, not influence the sensory-discriminative dimension. In the late 1960s, the three basic dimensions of pain marked an important advancement in therapy: pain can be treated not only by interrupting sensory information, for instance using anaesthetic blockade, or surgically, but also by influencing affective-motivational and cognitive factors.

In the late 1960s and early 1970s, W. E. Fordyce described the concept of pain behavior and the operant approach to treatment. At the beginning of the 1980s, D. C. Turk developed the cognitive-behavioral (CB) model of chronic pain. In the 1990s, based on the work of Turk and Salkovsky, chronic pain therapy began to integrate more and more cognitive therapy. The works by Fordyce and Turk also serve as a basis for Loeser's biopsychosocial model of pain (Loeser and Turk, 2001). Two groups of models are based on the concept of dimensions of pain by Melzack and Casey, the concept of pain behavior, and CBT development: models of gradual stages of change in chronic pain, and models emphasizing feedback processes in the development of psychological changes. Regarding models of gradual stages of change, a four-stage linear causal model was developed: 1. sensory-differentiating stage of pain, characterized by intensity; 2. affective stage 1 - characterized by feelings of unpleasantness and emotional annoyance; 3. affective stage 2, i.e. "suffering", the cognitively mediated stage of pain, leading to generalized changes in affects such as fear, anxiety, frustration, anger or depression; and 4.

apparent behavioral manifestations of pain (Wade and Hart, 2002). Models emphasizing feedback processes assume that if pain and pain evaluation lead to "catastrophizing" (a cognitive construct that involving the choice of unfavourable and threatening information, inducing strong fear, avoidance, and depression), an unfavourable development of the pain condition continues. If the evaluation of pain arouses low fear, it leads to adaptation and recovery (Vlayen et al., 2012). Psychological processes in chronic pain comprise both models of consecutive stages of change in chronic pain as well as models emphasizing feedback processes in the development of psychological changes.

Components of Pain

Each individual's perception of pain varies in all its domains (i.e. somatic, emotional, cognitive and behavioral). Therefore, besides the sensory aspect, pain also includes emotions, thoughts, behavior and social processes; a bidirectional causal relationship is applicable here. Pain is subjectively expressed by an individual in terms of intensity, quality and suffering (i.e. attitude to pain). In the somatic component of pain, the psychotherapist should focus on the words the patient uses to describe the quality of pain (pulsating, throbbing, stinging, shooting, burning, crampy pain); on the time aspect (how often the pain occurs); what the intensity of the pain is and how long the pain lasts. In order for the psychotherapist to better understand the emotional component of pain, he or she should ask the patient about his or her mood and emotions when experiencing the pain. The patient may feel anxious, frustrated, desperate, furious or depressed. Identification of emotions associated with pain is important, mainly for depression and situational anxiety, their duration and specific reactions to the fear of movement and pain. It may be very difficult for the patient to distinguish emotions from the somatic component of pain and emotional changes are often indicators of important shifts in thinking. Therefore, the therapist should also know what thoughts and basic beliefs are activated in an individual when he or she experiences pain, i.e. the cognitive component of pain. Chronic pain patients tend to have specific opinions and beliefs about pain, including how significantly pain affects their life as well as life of the others. For instance, they are unable to participate in work or daily activities, enter into relations with other people in an adequate way, have problems with their own role in the family and lose their identity. For these reasons they often have negative, unrealistic and catastrophic thoughts. For example, a patient with chronic pain thinks: "Pain has taken my life from me. I *cannot overcome the pain myself in any way. God is punishing me for my sins."* Catastrophic thoughts correlate with anxiety and the increased intensity of pain. Chronic pain patients are more vulnerable to catastrophic thoughts than, for example, depressive patients not suffering from pain (Winterowd et al., 2003). It is therefore important also to monitor any coping styles employed, for instance the extent of passivity and negative appraisal, the extent of catastrophic thinking and the ability to solve problems. It is also important for the psychotherapist to know what the patient does and how he or she behaves when suffering from chronic pain, which concerns the behavioral component of pain. Pain behavior represents the overt behavioral processes associated with pain, disability and the overall functioning of an individual. Some individuals may behave in very specific ways. Most of them, if they feel intense and persisting pain, try to avoid the pain: they often lie down and rest more often than normal, seeking relief. The fear of pain is more debilitating than the pain itself and often has a much higher intensity than the pain itself (Raudenska et al., 2013). Other patients may want to manage all the activities that they had before the pain, which leads to increased fatigue, pain and plan failure. Others may, only in order to alleviate the pain, overuse painkillers. This pain behaviour, in the broader sense of the word, requires the attention of not only the psychotherapist, but also of all the medical staff in the therapeutic team as well as other important people around the individual who may reinforce the pain behavior or the intensity of pain and suffering. That is why the therapist focuses on the impact of pain and its treatment on the general physical condition of the patient, changes in social roles and social functioning and behaviour related to health care provision – use of prescribed and over-the-counter drugs, the number of visits to the general practitioner, the number of visits to specialist physicians for a "second opinion", and regular as well as irregular visits to see a doctor at a Pain Management Centre (Morley et al., 1999).

As a patient's experience of pain is individual in all the above mentioned pain components, the therapeutic approach focuses on emotions, thoughts, opinions, beliefs, behavior and other somatic complaints. Therefore, the use of cognitive behavioral therapy (CBT) is dominant worldwide in the treatment of patients with chronic pain, altered mental states, irrational cognitive schemas and pain behavior.

APPROACHES

In the development of CBT in pain treatment, we may distinguish three basic approaches: behavioral (operant), cognitive and cognitive-behavioral. Behavioral approach. In the late 1970s, W. E. Fordyce published psychological methods in pain treatment based on behavioral methods (Fordyce, 1976). They focused on changes in behavior (relaxation, systematic desensitization, training in assertivity and social skills). Fordyce defined behavior as "observable and potentially measurable responses of an organism", thus, "observable movement". He compared behavior to the "dead man test": a dead man could not speak, cry or walk. If an individual's behavior was only observed, it was not sure whether or not he or she was thinking at the same time, whether he or she felt or did not feel sad, or if he or she felt or did not feel restless. For this reason, Fordyce defined speaking as behavior. Fordyce limited behavior to activity observable by others, excluding internal processes such as thinking or imagination. Notwithstanding, Fordyce's work comprised numerous innovations: he promoted pain behavior exposure and elimination of the behavior through ignoring, while reinforcing positive (healthy) behavior by praise/reward. Treatment involved eight weeks of hospitalization based on reduction of activity avoidance, aerobic, fitness and stretching exercises, and occupational therapy. He also described systematic pharmacologic therapy in pain management and integrated family into the treatment. Patients in Fordyce's studies showed an enormous increase in physical activity, a decrease in medication use and pain intensity in the active treatment phase. In the first stage, the studies did not have a control group, but control groups were included in the 1980s. Fordyce gradually oriented pain therapy to an outpatient form in which treatment duration was decreased to four weeks and patients were followed for two years. Not only did behavioral therapy decrease the intensity of pain, but it importantly increased social and work activities and pointed out the social aspects of chronic pain behavior (McCracken, 2005). Fordyce's operant approach emphasized the influence of learning on pain-related behavior, but for instance omitted certain somatic factors such as health status or cognitive factors such as the patient's expectations. In the 1970s, Fordyce and his colleagues drew attention to the possibilities of integrating psychotherapy to chronic pain management to a significant extent.

Cognitive-behavioral approach. In the 1970s and 1980s, cognitive therapy developed too. On the basis of works by Beck, Rush, and Shaw and Emery, D.C. Turk worked out the cognitive-behavioral (CB) model of chronic pain in the early 1980s (Turk et al., 1993). The aim was to unify useful methods from the behavioral approach and integrate methods from cognitive therapy. In pain management, the work represented a significant deflection from the operant approach represented by Fordyce in the 1970s. The basic assumptions of the cognitive-behavioral approach of Turk and his colleagues were: 1. emotions and behavior are influenced by the way in which the individual constructs his world; 2. therapy should help the patient identify and test reality and correct maladaptive, deformed and distorted belief. This allowed for work with the maladaptive thoughts that influence and maintain maladaptive behavior. Contrary to behavioral therapists who used external manipulation to change behavior, Turk and colleagues used manipulation as an information feedback experiment (behavioral experiment). This provided the patient with the possibility to ask, reappraise, review and gain control over his/her maladaptive cognition and feelings as well as behavior. The behavioral approach focused more on changing the patient's external environment with the aim of a change in behavior, the CB approach focused primarily, but not exclusively, on control and cognitive methods to achieve the desired change in mood and behavior. CBT advanced pain therapy in many ways: it brought focus on thoughts and feelings and their importance in the experience of pain; it helped patients focus on changes in behavior which may be initiated in the therapy through active cooperation and participation in treatment; applied skills to reduce pain and improve psychosocial functioning including fitness; defined attention, thoughts and patterns of behavior as the target for potential change. The patient's response to pain may include observable pain behavior, but also thoughts and images assessing situations associated with pain. These play an important role mainly in the event that the original harm that caused the pain is no longer present, or was not found at all by current diagnostic medical methods. Avoidance behavior may be encouraged by cognition. Anxiety and stress may reinforce the idea that "some damage" causing the pain does exist, which gives rise to cognitive errors, mistakes, negative appraisal and avoidance - the vicious circle remains. The CB model incorporates stress which may increase anxiety as well as pain behavior (Sharp, 2001). In CBT, individual methods are targeted at forms and frequency of thoughts and ideas, consequently leading to other changes in patient behavior. Thus, the changes in dysfunctional attitude are undoubtedly the causal mechanism of the treatment effect (Burns and Spangler, 2001).

In the 1990s, on the basis of the work of Turk and Salkovsky (focusing on the study of anxiety and depression in chronic pain), CB therapy of chronic pain starts to incorporate cognitive therapy to an increasing extent. The principle resides in the fact that people do not respond directly to stimuli from their surroundings, but to cognitive representations of this environment. The process of learning is based on the model of stimulus-organism-response-consequence. Cognitive processes have an intermediary function between the stimulus and behavior. It is not the stimulus (such as back pain) which induces certain behavior (I lie down, or I am lying down most of the day), but the meaning that the person attributes to the stimulus. The meaning of pain "I must lie down, otherwise it will get even worse and I will have to be operated on" leads to lying down on the bed and actually to pain relief, but gradually also to decreased activity and significant deterioration of the general musculoskeletal and cardiovascular condition. The consequences reinforce or weaken behavior, based on what meaning the person has attributed to the consequences. The key skills that chronic pain patients can learn during cognitive therapy include: identification and attenuation of the negative and unrealistic assessment of pain, of themselves, the world and the future, and the ability to solve problems (this will allow them to make decisions, complete tasks and set realistic life goals). Thanks to the knowledge and use of these skills, patients with chronic pain may experience pain less intensively, feel less emotional anxiety, improve their ability to cope with situations and have better relations with other people, including doctors and medical staff, colleagues, family members and friends. At the beginning of the 21st century, the synonym cognitive therapy starts to be used for CBT (Winterowd et al., 2003), even though, for instance, both the fully cognitive and behavioral approaches are advocated. Isolated use of cognitive or behavioral techniques, however, may limit the treatment of anxiety or depressive disorders that often accompany chronic pain. For example, behavioral treatment of anxiety disorders, including exposure, also produces changes in cognitive variables. Similarly, for example, analysis of CBT in depression shows that cognitive treatment strategies alone do not play an essential role in achieving change in automatic negative thoughts or dysfunctional schemas, and it is therefore advisable to apply behavioral techniques as well.

INDICATION FOR CBT

Patients who are referred for CB pain therapy are often in long-term incapacity for work or are already receiving social benefits, have decreased functional capacity, impaired social roles, experience chronic fatigue and often suffer from sleep disorders. After some time they become socially isolated and dissatisfied with their role in the family as well as with their competences. The patients rely too much on support provided by the social and health care system, which is intensified by the never-ending search for the second opinions of other doctors, repeated iatrogenic surgical solutions, and thus never-ending pain treatment (Sharpe and Bass, 1992). Perpetual attempts at adapting oneself to pain and its negative consequences often result in a number of emotional problems the most frequent of which are depression and fear associated with pain as well as other phobic responses (fear of social interaction, of leaving a safe environment, fear of blood, illness and death) (Asmundson et al., 1996). Chronic pain, fear and depression also have a negative impact on other cognitive functions: decreased focus of attention, worsened memory and increased failure in cognitive tasks (Estlander, 1996; Schnurr and MacDonald, 1995).

Thus, the individual, in an individual way, is always experiencing problems associated with pain treatment which influence suffering. These may be divided into four areas. Problems occurring in the area of personal problems include changes in understanding oneself and in self-appraisal, role loss, the depersonalization of the individual in the health care system and a continual search for medical care. In the domain of relational and social problems, conveying the subjective experience of pain to others has become the principal problem for the patient. The patient does not know what he or she can expect from the other people. This results in social isolation and renders the making of contacts more difficult. In the third area concerning philosophical and existential problems, the patient often asks him or herself questions such as: "Why me?", "What shall I do now?" and "What is the sense and meaning of life with chronic pain?". In the domain of spiritual problems, the patient, under the influence of chronic pain, reevaluates not only his/her faith, but also the general concept of spirituality. The individual problems of each individual in all the above mentioned areas affect how the patient will respond to treatment, how he or she will comply with treatment, how he or she will follow recommendations and what will the benefit be to his or her sense of life even with suffering and chronic pain.

Modeling the etiology and maintenance factors in the individual types of chronic pain is a challenge for further therapy (Soderlund and Lindberg, 2001). The narrow concept of CBT is therefore formed by behavioral analysis of the patient's problem. Cognitive behavioral therapy may be used as individual or group therapy. Individual CBT is short, structured therapy consisting of up to 5-10 sessions. The therapist is always active and directive in conducting this therapy, seeking the client's active cooperation.

The broad concept of CBT in pain management is represented by holistic programs conducted by a multidisciplinary team. Treatment involves group therapy, combined psychotherapy, pharmacotherapy and physiotherapy and patients are hospitalized in Pain Management Centres for 2-4 weeks, the treatment may also be conducted on an outpatient basis. Without the possibility of an interdisciplinary team, treatment inefficiency increases because patients are looking for a "cure" for their pain (i.e., its removal or alleviation) (Loeser, 1996). This cannot be wondered at. For this reason, treatment is primarily focused on reducing the undesirable impact of chronic pain on life, that is, on improving the quality of life, and not on decreasing or removing the pain. Indications for CBT are: 1. the patient suffers from unmanageable chronic pain, 2. The pain affects the patient's emotional status, or the emotional status worsens the pain intensity, 3. The patient has difficulty coping with pain and treatment (e.g. a problematic relationship between the doctor and the patient, the patient is afraid of being examined or of therapy, he or she exacts it, or refuses it), 4. The patient faces a stressful situation of a psychosocial nature (tense relations with family and friends, physical limitations disabling the patient from performing common tasks and activities independently), has lost his or her job or has serious financial problems. CBT may be contraindicated in chronic pain patients for serious cognitive deficits, lack of interest and motivation, or if the patients are acutely psychotic at the time of treatment initiation. These patients may benefit from behavioral interventions or supportive psychotherapy. Some patients may desire a different type of psychotherapy from the very start. It is therefore important for the therapist to present the CB treatment properly to the patients before initiation, to explain the techniques and principles as well as its effectiveness in detail. Patients who complete tasks frequently and use the CBT techniques achieve best results in long-term follow-up. Patients who refuse to accept the principles of CBT (homework, records, diaries etc.) as part of pain management, insist on an unrealistic goals for the therapy *("It must never hurt again!")*, or have very low motivation, will not benefit from the treatment. The team should also consider the use of CBT in patients who have already undergone it.

TECHNIQUES

The basic steps in KB therapy are the following: 1. preliminary examination; 2. detailed examination; 3. behavioral, cognitive and functional analysis of the problem, verbalization and definition of the problem; 4. goals of the therapy, evaluation of existing pain coping skills; 5. therapy: creating a therapeutic plan, teaching of new skills, pain relapse prevention; 6. end of therapy; 7. aftercare and follow-up. Chronic pain management uses two fundamental approaches that will be described below: cognitive restructuring and training in pain and stress coping skills (Turner and Romano, 2001).

1. Cognitive restructuring. Chronic pain patients can have unrealistic and negative beliefs and opinions about their pain, themselves, the world and their future. It is therefore important to focus on identifying, evaluating and modifying negative thoughts, images and expectations in the following four areas. 1. pain beliefs: patients with chronic pain may develop a global view on how pain has affected their lives. Many patients enter therapy with negative expectations. Examples: *"My pain is untreatable. I cannot control my pain in any way. The pain is horrible and unbearable. My life is full of pain, the pain has taken all of my past life from me. Nothing and no-one, not even you, can help me anymore, in any way."* 2. beliefs about self: in a person suffering from chronic pain, his or her perception of their identity may change over time. Some patients, for instance, may not be able to return to their original work because their profession was a physically demanding one. Examples of such beliefs include: *"My pain has made me a weak person. I am vulnerable. I am powerless. The pain is useless for me. I cannot be helped any more"*. Patients may also develop various beliefs about their own body. For example: *"My body is completely broken. I am not functioning any longer. I have grown old. I am crippled"*. 3. beliefs about the world: some patients begin to think more, asking themselves questions concerning their relationships with others that have changed as a result of their chronic pain. Although being treated, they are impatient, affecting relationships not only with the medical team, but also with their partners and family. Some of them believe that others will reject them because of their physical limitations and pain. Examples of negative beliefs about the world include: *"My doctor does not care about me and is not treating me; I should have been pain-free long ago. No one can understand what I am going through. People will criticize me. The world is against me. People are disappointed in me."* 4. beliefs about the future: patients imagine how bad and gloomy their future with chronic pain will be. Examples of beliefs about the future include: *"My future looks grim. All I can see ahead of me is pain."* Negative and unrealistic thoughts and images contribute to physical and emotional suffering as well as to self-destructive behaviors. With irrational thinking and evaluation of pain, the individual has a greater tendency to develop a negative self-image, and negative views of the world and the future, which leads to feelings of despair, powerlessness and, through a vicious circle, to the worsening of symptoms. If, under the influence of chronic pain, dysfunctional schemas are activated in a pre-disposed individual, this may manifest as the occurrence of automatic negative thoughts (ANTs). These do not assess reality objectively, but in a distorted way *("I cannot do anything with pain")*. A chronic pain patient who has a tendency for ANTs *("The pain is horrible, and it will never be better. I will be end up in a wheelchair anyway!")* will benefit from cognitive restructuring. It is necessary to explain to the patient that emotional responses to pain are influenced by his or her thinking. ANTs may also be a direct response to an increase in pain intensity: *"Something is wrong, something wrong is happening to me.", "The pain will end with hospitalization and another operation."* If the patient understands the relation between thoughts and emotions, learns to identify ANTs, evaluate them and find alternative, "reasonable" answers, it affects the emotional and behavioral as well as the somatic components of pain.

2. Coping with pain and stress helps the patient build up a repertoire of skills for effective coping. This includes the techniques of education, self-instruction, relaxation, activity increase, exposure, problem solving, relapse coping etc. Education by a doctor, nurse, psychologist or physiotherapist usually forms part of a comprehensive pain treatment plan (Williams and Harding, 1995). It starts with topics about diagnoses that are associated with chronic pain (back pain, arthritis, complex regional pain syndrome, orofacial pain, headaches, etc.), and further continues with causes of the occurrence of pain, the role of diagnostic and therapeutic approaches, explanation of the biopsychosocial model of chronic pain (somatic and psychosocial factors during the onset and maintenance of pain), and the relationship between stress, tension and pain. Education leads to a better understanding of the patient's own problems with chronic pain. Adaptive positive self-instruction means managing increased pain or stress with adaptive thoughts based on the principle of self-suggestion, for example: *"I will cope with this!", "Focus on relaxation!", "Tension is here for me to use my coping skills!", "This won't last long, take it easy, you will manage this!"*. The patient is told that anxiety and tension can increase pain as well as focusing attention on pain. The level of anxiety is influenced by the way in which the person assesses the unpleasant experience with pain at a given moment, for example: *"Will I manage this?", "This is horrible, I can't bear the pain!"* It is therefore also possible to decrease the anxiety and tension by thought replacement. Self-instruction is helpful in all stages of pain management: 1. in preparation for pain: *"Think of what you can do, worrying and fear will not help reduce the pain!"*, 2. when confronting unpleasant feelings: *"I can think of something more pleasant than pain!"*, the 3rd stage involves managing intense pain: *"I can manage any pain with correct breathing and relaxation. I can manage this, I will pull through it!"*, 4. in the final stage, self-instruction is used when looking back: *"I managed it well, good job!"*. Relaxation and imagination. Patients who respond to stress with increased anxiety, muscle tension and pain may benefit from relaxation. With regular relaxation, the patient may achieve a reduction in stress, tension and pain, a distraction of attention from pain and improvement in sleep. Increasing activity. The patient uses diaries to record all activities (the belief that he or she "does not do anything, cannot manage anything with the pain" is thus challenged), recording at the same time what mood he or she was in and how he or she enjoyed the activity. The next step is the planning of activities for the following day and gradual inclusion of activities that he or she does not enjoy so much. That modifies thoughts such as *"I am good for nothing with the pain"* or *"I cannot manage anything with the pain!"*. In chronic pain patients, a gradual increase in activities is combined with rehabilitation; body building and stretching exercise are used, exercise is gradually intensified (*pacing*), and exposure is thereby employed at the same time. Mastery of each step is reinforced with rewards. Exposure. Exposure in vivo is most suitable for reducing fear of pain and movement. First of all we measure the fear, find out in which situations it occurs, explain how fear develops and how it manifests in the somatic, cognitive and behavioral domain. We focus on the particular problem of the patient in connection with pain: for example, fear of riding an exercise bike, of bending forward, fear of rehabilitation exercise etc. With the patient, we line up the feared situations in a hierarchy from the simplest to the most difficult, and using exposure we escalate the difficulty. The patient himself or herself will set up the goal of therapy, revised by the therapist, for instance: to walk the dog in the park every day at 3:10 p.m. without any fear of pain, manage to talk to other people during this, smile and be in a good mood etc. The PHODA (Photograph Series of Daily Activities) method can be advised to be used for the diagnosis and planning of exposure in vivo therapy in patients with pain-related fear (Kugler et al., 1999). Chronic pain patients also benefit from anxiety treatment. We can intentionally provoke anxiety symptoms and subsequently teach the patient to relax: in this way he or she will find out that the consequences he or she is afraid of (*"My back aches, I cannot exercise, or I will end up on an operating table, I will go crazy...!")* will not follow. Gradually, we may provoke positions, situations or behaviors that provoke increased anxiety in the patient and, with the help of other techniques such as cognitive restructuring or self-instruction, anxiety can be reduced. This should be performed with the assistance of a rehabilitation doctor or physiotherapist. Reduction in anxiety allows patients to rehabilitate effectively. Structured problem solving. Improvement in the ability to solve problems leads to a decrease in the overall level of anxiety. Preparing the patient for relapse (increasing the intensity of pain, anxiety or depression). At the beginning of therapy, patients often have unrealistic expectancies about getting rid of pain forever, but an increase in pain, anxiety or depression may occur in the course of as well as after the end of therapy. Unrealistic expectancies such as *"The pain will never reappear!"* may result in disappointment, and the pessimistic *"I will never get rid of the pain, no one will ever help me!"* leads to depression. It is therefore necessary to identify all behaviors, emotions, thoughts and physiological reactions with an impact on increasing pain intensity. The therapist and the patient will cooperate to identify the "red flags", i.e., situations that were associated with an increased intensity of pain or stress in the past. Adaptive relapse coping comprises two parts: 1. preparation for an increased intensity of pain and 2. strategies used at the time of increased pain.

MULTIDISCIPLINARY PROGRAM

CBT is organised in pain management centres of the highest level as a multidisciplinary pain management program conducted by a team of experts (anesthesiologist, clinical psychologist, physiotherapist, nurse) trained in CBT. All members of the team have equal status. The whole multidisciplinary pain management team meets to evaluate current problems, the course of the programme and the treatment; they also meet with every new patient following the initial and complex algesiological, psychological, physiotherapeutic examination and occupational counseling to evaluate the expected effect of treatment and motivation for the patient's participation in the program; they also meet with every patient once a week for treatment evaluation, and, as needed, to communicate with doctors who recommended the patients for the program. The programs vary in content and duration and are adapted to groups of individuals with a particular diagnosis (headaches, back pain, fibromyalgia, rheumatoid arthritis). The accessibility of multidisciplinary pain management programs is limited by the financial situation of the health care system and by the staff who should undergo training in CBT. In therapy, it is not the concrete contents of each individual session of the programme that is important, but the factors structuring the therapy. The basic factors that are preconditions for a successful multidisciplinary pain management program are described below.

Direct positive reinforcement of pain behavior. The overall apparent behavior of the individual (tone and contents of verbal expression, gait and posture, facial expression, and medical care utilization) gives others information about pain. The consequences of pain behavior are harmful to the patients themselves and increase their suffering. CBT is therefore focused on situations at home, at work and in healthcare institutions where the patient is directly reinforced for pain-related behavior. For example: a patient may leave work whenever she suffers from headache. If a patient feels the onset of back pain, he does not have to participate in household duties and goes to bed. Moaning and crying at the doctor's office due to pain always results in an increased level of care from the doctor, the nurse puts the patient on a bed, measures his or her blood pressure, the doctor devotes more time to the patient, or the patient is kept at the day care centre for monitoring. CBT seeks to minimize these effects.

Indirect positive reinforcement of pain behavior. Avoidance behavior is the most common form of reinforcement of pain and disability. The patient will avoid pain in situations which provoke the pain because he or she believes that the pain is reduced by avoiding it. Avoidance behavior, however, actually increases the intensity of pain. The patient develops a constant pattern of activity: he or she is active when feeling good and less active if he or she feels higher pain intensity. After a certain time, this pattern inevitably leads to a stable decline in activity. In the course of CBT, the maladaptive patterns of avoidance behavior are replaced by encouraging the patient to exhibit time-contingent behavior (for instance, to change their position every 15 minutes from sitting to standing and vice versa) and draw up plans for attainable goals. Every success is reinforced by reward (Eccleston, 2001).

Positive reinforcement of required behavior. Insufficient reinforcement of healthy behavior inhibits and reduces mental well-being. CBT therefore focuses on identification and reinforcement of healthy (adaptive) behavior and encourages patients in adaptive behavior. Family members are also trained in how to react to an individual's needs and how to appreciate his or her balanced physical as well as emotional state.

Physical condition. A chronic pain patient is lying down or sitting all day long and starts to realise that he or she does not function physically: the person is more and more tired and loses breath even during minimum activity (walking one floor upstairs). However, he or she perceives these problems as pain-related and potentially harmful. Improvement in general physical condition can reduce tiredness as well as other somatic symptoms, including pain. It is often the increase in physical condition that represents the first positive reinforcement for a patient in CBT.

Cognitive reframing. Patients are steered towards discovering the automatic nature of negative, catastrophizing and self-degrading thinking patterns. Subsequently, they test the substantiality of these thinking patterns and assumptions that these thoughts are based on. In this way, the impact of thoughts on emotions and vice versa is understood. Cognitive restructuring is performed along with the teaching of communication skills, identification of problems and their solution, stress management and relaxation training.

Education and reinforcement. Education provides directions for the patient to be able to understand pain and to influence it to a certain extent. Thus, it reduces the emotional and evaluative component of pain (Strong and Unruh, 2003).

Besides the above six therapeutic principles, there are other factors that influence the process of therapy success. Therapy needs to be conducted in a structured way and on the basis of consistent CB principles. Therapy will be more effective if all staff members of the Pain Management Centre are trained in CBT, the team is regularly supervised and if there is no need to assure stable pharmacotherapy – changes in the middle of the CBT program may negatively affect the development of adaptive self-reinforcement and self-instruction behavior.

EFFECTIVENESS

CBT has been applied in a number of diagnoses: back pain, headaches, fibromyalgia, rheumatoid arthritis, orofacial pain and others. CBT in pain management represents, in comparison with control groups and groups of patients on the waiting list, the most effective tool to help remove impaired cognitive schemas, teaches adaptive behavior and coping, reduces pain behavior, anxiety, fear and catastrophic interpretation of somatic symptoms, increases activity and self-confidence and improves social roles (Flor et al., 1992; Eccleston et al., 2002; Turner et al., 1996; Turner et al., 2007). A systematic assessment of 33 controlled studies of CBT in adults (not including headaches) also showed a permanent reduction in pain intensity (Morley et al., 1999).

CBT effectiveness is related to the structure of CBT, multidisciplinary programs and also with the competences and training of the entire team in CBT. On the other hand, neither standards for CBT in chronic pain treatment, nor therapy audits exist. Effectiveness is negatively influenced by the variability of chronic pain states (headaches, back pain, joint pain…); small or different patient sample sizes; different time course of therapy (5 to 6 sessions on average, but ranging from 3 to 15); variability in the CB techniques used as well as of statistical processing (Keefe and Van Horn, 1993; Parker et al., 1993). The effects of therapy may be positively influenced by familiarizing the patient with CBT effectiveness prior to treatment: patients with multiple diagnoses (Basler and Rehfisch, 1990), with headaches (Gutkin et al., 1992), or mixed pain (Parker et al., 1988) who were motivated for treatment showed more significant improvements than patients who were forced to undergo treatment. Thus, effectiveness of CBT increases when the attending physician, or the family encourage the patient to undergo psychotherapy. CBT may not be effective in patients whose health condition is complicated by court proceedings or by enforcement of compensation and social benefits, in addicted patients or patients whose pain behavior is reinforced by their domestic environment. CBT is more effective if applied in the early phase of chronic pain and if it is a part of a multidisciplinary program.

CBT has its limitations, too, which have an impact on its effectiveness: some chronic pain patients, although well selected and motivated, do not benefit from the treatment; we cannot predict with absolute certainty which patients will be helped by CBT and which will not; the specific mechanisms of the therapy remain unknown in some cases, and in many parts of the world, CBT is not available at the time of need, or is not available at all. Further research faces the challenge of rethinking whether chronic pain therapy should be focused on the analgesic effect or rather on the rehabilitation process (Morley et al., 2013). Therapy should be based on an explicit theoretical model that leads to the selection of therapeutic techniques, the extent and quality of care, the methodological quality of the studies and standard statistical processing.

Conclusion

The operant approach opened the possibility of managing pain as a behavior problem (in relation to the patient's external environment) and stimulated the development of behavioral methods. The cognitive behavioral approach introduced the investigation of mental processes, and therapeutic methods focused on the modification of thinking and images to improve emotional and behavioral functioning. Current CB pain therapy is holistic, structured and targeted at the individual's quality of life. Patients learn the basic skills for managing pain as well as pain-related psychosocial problems. Effectiveness of CBT has been shown in all the modalities of pain (static, emotional, cognitive and behavioral). CBT should therefore be an integral part of chronic pain management.

References

Asmundson, G. J. G., Norton, G. R. & Jacobson, S. J. (1996). Social, blood/injury, and agoraphobic fears in patients with physically unexplained chronic pain-are they clinically significant? *Anxiety*, *2*, 28-33.

Basler, H. & Rehfisch, H. (1990). Follow-up results of a cognitive-behavioural treatment for chronic pain in primary care setting. *Psychology and Health*, *4*, 293-304.

Burns, D. D. & Spangler, D. L. (2001). Do dysfunctional attitudes mediate recovery from depression and anxiety in cognitive behavioral therapy? *Behavior Therapy*, *32*, 337-369.

Eccleston, C. H. (2001). Role of psychology in pain management. *British Journal of Anaesthesia*, *1*, 144-152.

Eccleston, C. & Crombez, G. (1999). Pain demands attention: a cognitive-affective model of the interruptive function of pain. *Psychol Bull*, *3*, 356-366.

Eccleston, C. H., Morely, S. & Williams, A. (2002). Systematic review of randomised controlled trials of psychological therapy for chronic pain in children and adolescents, with a subset meta analysis of pain relief. *Pain*, *99*, 157-165.

Estlander, A. (1996). Assessment of Cognitive Variables and Depression in Patients with Chronic Pain. In Campbell, J. (Ed.), *Pain 1996 – an Updated Review* (505-512). Seattle: IASP Press.

Flor, H., & Fydrich, T. & Turk, D. C. (1992). Efficacy of multidisciplinary pain treatment centers: a meta-analytic review. *Pain*, *49*, 221–230.

Fordyce, W. E. (1976). *Behavioral methods for chronic pain and illness*. St. Louis: Mosby.

Gutkin, A., Holborn, S., Walker, J. & Anderson, B. (1992). Treatment integrity of relaxation training for tension headache. *Journal of Behavioral Therapy and Experimental Psychiatry*, *23*, 191-198.

Keefe, F. & Van Horn, Y. (1993). Cognitive-behavioral-tretament of rheumatoid arthritis pain. *Arthritis Care and Research*, *6*, 213-222.

Kugler, K., Wijn, J., Grilem, M., de Jong, J., Heuts, P. H. & Vlaeyen, J. W. S. (1999). *The photograf series of Daily Activities, PHODA, CD-rom version.* Maastricht: Institute for Rehabilitaiton Research Hoensbroek, School of Physiotherapy Heerlen and Maastricht University.

Loeser, J. D. (1996). Mitigating the dangers of pursuing cure. In Cohen, M.J.M., & Campbell, J.N. (Ed.), *Pain Treatment Centers at a Crossroads: A Practical and Conceptual Reappraisal* (101–108). Seattle: IASP Press.

Loeser, J. & Turk, D. (2001). Multidisciplinary Pain Management. In Loeser, J. (Ed.), *Bonica´s Management of Pain* (2067-2079). Philadelphia: Lippincott Williams and Wilkins.

Melzack, R. & Wall, P. D. (1965). Pain mechanisms: a new theory. *Science*, *150*, 971–979.

Melzack, R. & Casey, K. L. (1968). Sensory, motivational and central control determinants of chronic pain: A new conceptual model. In Kenshalo, D.R. (Ed.), *The Skin Senses* (430-440). Springfield Illinois: Thomas.

McCracken, L. (2005). *Contextual Cognitive-Behavioral Therapy for Chronic Pain.* Seattle: IASP Press.

Morley, S. & Eccleston, C. & Williams, A. (1999). Systematic review and meta-analysis of randomised controlled trials of cognitive behaviour therapy and behaviour therapy for chronic pain in adults, excluding headache. *Pain*, *80*, 1–13.

Morley, S., & Williams, A. & Eccleston, C. (2013). Examining the evidence about psychological treatments for chronic pain: Time for paradigm shift? *Pain*, *154*, 1929–1931.

Parker, J., Frank, R., Beck, N., Smarr, K., Buescher, K., Philips, L., Smith, E., Anderson, S. & Walker, S. (1988). Pain management in rheumatoid arthritis patients: A cognitive-behavioral approach. *Arthritis and Rheumatis*, *31*, 593-601.

Parker, J., Iverson, G., Smarr, K. & Stucky-Ropp, R. (1993). Cognitive-behavioral approaches to pain management in rheumatoid arthritis. *Arthritis Care and Research*, *6*, 207-212.

Price, D. D. (1999). Psychological Mechanisms of Pain and Analgesia (*Progress in Pain Research and Management*, V. *15*). Seattle, WA: IASP Press.

Price, D. D. & Harkins, S. W. (1992). The *affective*-motivational dimension of pain: a two stage model. *APS J*, *1*, 229 -239.

Raudenska, J., Javurkova, A. & Kozak, J. (2013). Fear of pain and movement in a patient with musculoskeletal chronic pain. *Neuronedocrinol Lett*, *6*, 101-104.

Sharp, T. (2001). Chronic pain: a reformulation of the CB model. *Behaviour Research and Therapy*, *39*, 787-800.

Sharpe, M. & Bass, C. (1992). Pathophysiological mechanisms in somatization. *Int Rev Psychiatry*, *4*, 81–97.

Schnurr, R. F. & MacDonald, M. R. (1995). Memory complaints in chronic pain. *Clin J Pain*, *11*, 103–111.

Soderlund, A. & Lindberg, P. (2001). An Integrated Physiotherapy/Cognitive-Behavioural Approach to the Analysis and Treatment of Chronic Whiplash Associated Disorders, WAD. *Disabil Rehabil*, *10*, 436-447.

Spielberger, C. D., Ritterband, L. M., Reheiser, E. C. & Brunner, T.M. (2003). The nature and measurement of depression. *International Journal of Clinical and Health Psychology*, 3, 209-234.

Strong, J. & Unruh, A. M. (2003). Psychologically based pain management strategies. In Strong, J., & Unruh, A.M., & Wright, A., & Baxter, G.D. (Ed.), *Pain. A textbook for therapists* (169-186). London: Elsevier Science Limited.

Turk, D. C., Rudy, T. E. & Sorkin, B. A. (1993). Neglected topics in chronic pain treatment outcome studies-determination of success. *Pain*, *53*, 3–16.

Turner, J., Schroth, W. S. & Fordyce, W. E. (1996). Educational and behavioural interventions for back pain in primary care. *Spine*, *21*, 2851–2859.

Turner, J. & Romano, J. (2001). Cognitive-Behavioral Therapy for Chronic Pain. In Loeser, J. (Ed.), *Bonica´s Management of Pain* (1751-1758). Philadelphia: Lippincott Williams & Wilkins.

Turner A. T., Holtzman, S. & Mancl, L. (2007). Mediators, moderators, and predictors of therapeutic change in cognitive-behavioral therapy for chronic pain. *Pain*, *127*, 276-286.

Vlaeyen, J. W. S., Morley, S., Linton, S. J., Boersma, K. & de Jong, J. (2012). *Pain-Related Fear: Exposure-Based Treatment for Chronic Pain.* Seattle: IASP Press.

Wade, J. B. & Hart, R. P. (2002). Attention and the Stages of Pain processing. *Pain Med*, *3*, 30-38.

Wade, J. B., Dougherty, L. M., Archer, C. R. & Price, D. D. (1996). Assessing of stages of pain processing: a multivariate approach. *Pain*, *68*, 157-167.

Williams, A. & Harding, V. (1995). Applying Psychology to Enhance Physiotherapy Outcome. *Physiotherapy Theory and Practice*, *3*, 129-132.

Winterowd, C., Beck, A. T. & Gruener, D. (2003). *Cognitive Therapy with Chronic Pain Patients.* New York: Springer Publishing Co.

Reviewed by: Prof. Jan Prasko, MD, PhD. Chief of Department of Psychiatry, University Hospital Olomouc, Faculty of Medicine and Dentistry, University Palacky Olomouc, Czech Republic

In: Cognitive Behavioral Therapy
Editor: Brendan Myers
ISBN: 978-1-63321-638-9

Chapter 5

COGNITIVE BEHAVIORAL THERAPY FOR RHEUMATOID ARTHRITIS

Adriana Cardoso Silva*[1*]*, Ph.D,
***Alexandre Rafael de Mello Schier*[2]**
***and Natalia Pinho de Oliveira Ribeiro*[2]**
Institute of Psychiatry, Federal University of Rio de Janeiro, Brazil

ABSTRACT

Rheumatoid arthritis (RA) is an autoimmune, chronic, degenerative, progressive and disabling disease that affects about 1% of world population. RA patients suffer from persistent pain with acute attacks during crises. In addition, they also present stiffness, swelling, and loss of mobility due to inflammation of the joints. There are also less common symptoms such as fever, weakness, loss of appetite and sleepiness alteration. The most commonly damaged joints are knees, feet, hands, wrists, elbows, neck and the temporomandibular region, which are affected during the disease progression causing severe deformities, osteoarthritis, tendon rupture and decrease of the life expectancy of the patient in five to ten years. Besides, psychiatric comorbidities such as anxiety, depression and risk of suicide and para-suicide, have high prevalence in RA affecting the prognosis of RA and worsening the overall picture and the intensity of pain as well as compromising the

[*] Contact: Adriana Cardoso Silva, Ph.D. Professor and Researcher, Medical School – Institute of Psychiatry, Federal University of Rio de Janeiro. E-mail: adrianacardosorj@ufrj.br

ability of adherence to treatment. Cognitive-Behavioral Therapy for RA patients seeks not only the reduction of psychiatric comorbidities, such as anxiety and depression, for which this therapeutic model has already proved effective, but also for resolving specific issues of the clinical course of RA. Dysfunctional thoughts related to physical changes, deformities and body image perception are evaluated and restructured when necessary, as well as problem solving techniques are applied to identify new forms of everyday functioning, facilitating de rehabilitation of the patient considering the existence of physical limitations. Psychoeducation is useful to equip the patient to meet the challenges arising from the progress of the disease, and also the medical treatment. Pain control techniques are used to help patients to recognize and management the stimulus and situations that can worsening or reduce pain. New behaviors are developed to enable the performance of daily activities, considering the limitations imposed by the disease. With new coping behaviors, the patient starts to develop new thoughts about the disease, of him and of the future. Thus, it becomes possible to have a higher quality of life. Here we present a literature review on the topic, as well as a proposal for cognitive-behavioral treatment for RA considering its clinical challenges and, finally, are presented a case report.

INTRODUCTION

Rheumatoid arthritis (RA), as well as other diseases related to joints, has been noted by medicine since antiquity. The first mention of RA in an Ebers Papyrus, written around 1500 BC, which clearly described a condition similar to the disease; in Indian literature [1] Charak Samhita (written around 300 to 200 BC), the author reported about a condition similar to RA with symptoms of pain, inflammation of joints and loss of mobility by the stiffness of the joints. Hippocrates was the one who discovered and identified Arthritis (general symptoms) in 400 BC, however, he never came to define its various types.

RA is an autoimmune, inflammatory, and chronic disabling disease that affects the joints with its main reflections in the synovial, with symmetrical pattern and clear symptoms. RA causes pain, stiffness, swelling, loss of joint movement [2], and other not common symptoms like fever, weakness and loss of appetite. The joints constantly most affected by RA are knees, feet, hands, wrists, elbows, shoulders, temporomandibular joints and cervical spine region. During the disease, typically, the most common complications are progressive deformities, loss of function of the affected area, detrition of the joints (arthrosis), tendon rupture, cervical spine instability, and reduced life expectancy of the individual in five to ten years [3].

Despite being a joint disease, RA for being a systemic disease has the potential to involve almost every organ of the body and may present its course a progressive worsening of the picture, generalized osteoporosis, fatigue, thrombocytosis, hypergammaglobulinemia, pulmonary, hepatic lesions, alteration in lipid metabolism associated with atherogenesis (which is linked to systemic inflammatory diseases) may explain higher prevalence of coronary disease in these patients (which is the major cause of death in this group of patients, further enhanced by traditional risk factors such as smoking and obesity), anemia and stimulation of the hypothalamic hypophyseal leading to produce stress hormones like cortisol [4 – 5].

The RA is considered a very common disease, it is estimated to affect 0.2% to 1% of the Brazilian population [6]. It is estimated that at least 10% of the general complaints of joint pain can be attributed to the RA. Although is characterized by uncertain epidemiological data, one study [2] demonstrated that women are twice more affected than men, and its incidence increases with age; with a higher frequency in individuals between 50 and 70 years old.

Conventional pharmacological treatment of RA is intended for relieve its signs and symptoms (mainly inflammation, swelling and pain), minimize joint damage, maintain function and improve quality of life of patients by reducing premature mortality associated with this condition. So the main objective of the treatment is to suppress inflammation, which means in the final analysis, obtain remission. It is recommended [7] repeated evaluation of the patient with objective criteria to define the degree of improvement in each medical appointment in comparison to primary goal of disease remission to the maintenance and absolute control of the RA. Medical intervention includes everything from painkillers to nonsteroidal anti-inflammatory drug (NSAID), corticosteroids and drugs known as DMARDs (disease-modifying antirheumatic drugs) which are divided into synthetic (methotrexate, sulfasalazine, leflunomide, hidroxichloroquine).

In general, patients diagnosed with RA evolve with possibility of presenting concomitants psychopathology, not always detectable by nonpsychiatric doctors once they are no trained in psychopathology. As the disease progresses in severity and treatments deepen such impairments become more severe too. Furthermore, patients with chronic pain tend to develop psychiatric comorbidities. The acute and constant pain they feel can generate since suicidal thoughts to lead to the act itself [8 – 9].

Depression and anxiety present in patients with RA may also be explained by progressive autoimmune origin of it, which probable worsening with the onset of deformities, limitations and even irreversible disabilities, which ultimately generate the need for adaptation and permanent coexistence, thus excluding expectations regarding cure or improvement [10]. Within this picture it can also point to the possibility of comorbid symptoms that are caused or aggravated by the use of drugs with severe side effects, such as, for example, corticosteroids included in the treatment that often causes depression in patients. Other side effects such as swelling, change in appetite, sleep shifts and mood, the patient may also develop new diseases or symptoms that the individual and will also have to adapt.

Other lines of research [11] state that rheumatoid arthritis is a chronic disease, and, by itself would print its consequences to the patient. We can define as chronic disease a prolonged clinical abnormality that has the ability to change the social, psychological and physical activities of the individual affected, in various levels of intensity [12]. Such diseases, often disabling, may generate psychiatric disorders: by changing the brain functions, causing psychological or causing psychosocial bad influence on these functions, since it change the working routine or integrative activities of this individual in society.

The extensive knowledge of the clinical picture of RA, involving its diagnosis, common signs and symptoms, possibilities of drug treatment and their consequences, medical procedures commonly performed, clinical course and potential physiological outcomes arising from the aforementioned variables is essential for the therapist cognitive behavior. Only after this global understanding he can select the best techniques for working with this patient considering the particularities of the disease. More than that, the psychotherapist needs a deep understanding of how RA changes, day by day, these patients' bodies and life in general, besides the rehabilitation efforts required.

It is known that in chronic illness, physical and psychological distress follow interlaced, one affecting the other in a way that both of the RA picture is a potential generator of psychopathology conditions, these kinds of changes are able to worsen the prognosis regarding the evolution of the physical symptoms. In RA, besides the already mentioned high prevalence of mood-changes and anxiety, there are more subtle issues such as loss of autonomy caused by reduced mobility of this patient, which in some cases becomes extremely dependent on an external caregiver. Still, there is loss of work capacity, the potential for injury and even recreational restrictions, with the evolution of the overall picture of the disease, even as to perform simple everyday tasks such as dressing (mainly garments requiring final movements as close zippers and buttons) and even food (proper handling of cutlery). Thus, is evident the presence of deprivation in the social life aspect, in this case not only by physical limitations, but because of the avoidance of situations involving contact with other people due to discomfort with his own image, often marked by deformities of limbs affected.

Another delicate point is the pharmacotherapy, since the necessary drugs to control the disease are accompanied by many unpleasant side effects, including facilitating many depressive disorders once depression can be caused by excessive use of corticosteroids. Thus the psychotherapist needs to understand clearly what these effects are in order to assist the patient in the required treatment adherence, considering all the aspects involved including the predominance of psychological conditions according to the used chemical treatment [13]. It is important the psychotherapist who works with chronic diseases has good integration with other health professionals involved in the treatment and monitoring of patients in a transdisciplinary basis in the best interest of that under their care. Still, it is essential that, in addition to conventional environment (office or inner tire), the therapist is equipped to perform interventions, when necessary, also in the hospital environment, whenever the patient required hospitalization. The therapist should also be prepared to assist in specific medical procedures even when they occur in intensive treatment units.

Cognitive Behavioral Therapy for Medical Problems

Cognitive behavioral therapy (CBT) is a form of objective, directive and focal therapy, considered of short duration in which is valued active participation where patient and therapist work together as a team. Therapeutic approach assumes that cognitive elements influence behavior and that would be possible to monitor or alter these cognitive factors. Further, since the cognitive factors change, behaviors and feelings associated with them are also changed.

The model of therapy is educational and directive, moreover, evidence-based practices are appreciated. Its development is based on empirical knowledge, and the procedures and techniques are scientifically tested before being widely adopted as a regular clinical practice, providing greater patient safety and ensuring best results.

The usual procedure in CBT involve the formulation of the problem presented by the patient, development of therapeutic alliance, check automatic thoughts (AT), records of daily thoughts (RDTs) and subsequent verification of the them, definition and initiation of treatment of the symptoms that most disturb patients progressing to those that generate less discomfort, work dissociative beliefs and application of behavioral techniques, and facilitating adherence to treatment as much psychotherapeutic, medical and pharmacological one.

The efficacy of CBT has been tested since its creation in the 60s by Aaron Beck. Initially more focused on treatment of psychopathology and mental disorders like depression, Generalized Anxiety Disorder (GAD), Panic Disorder (PD), Social anxiety disorder (SAD), Obsessive Compulsive Disorder (OCD), Bipolar Disorder [14], Attention Deficit Hyperactivity Disorder (ADHD) when combined with medication, eating disorders, varying impulse disorders, Post Traumatic Stress Disorder (PTSD), among others, the CBT has expanded its borders to the development of therapeutic proposals for specific populations considering its particularities (elderly, children, families, couples) and even health problems.

The psychological support in other medical specialties other than psychiatry is gaining more space between the studies developed with this approach. There are proposals among them for intervention in pain syndromes, chronic and terminal illnesses and other diseases limiter and which generates dependency, progressive diseases and also degenerative diseases [15], minimizing not only comorbid psychiatric symptoms as well as the negative effects caused by illness in patients such as fatigue, increased levels of stress, pain control, increased frustration tolerance, change in body image, problem solving, planning and control techniques anxiety, stress, anger, among others, thus increasing the quality of life of each patient.

A CBT protocol for the treatment of patients with irritable bowel syndrome [16], for example, could reduce intestinal symptoms (diarrhea and abdominal pain), encouraging more adaptive coping strategies, reducing avoidance behaviors and psychological symptoms also improving the perception patient's quality of life. In patients with chronic pain syndromes and no chance of cure CBT has also been shown to be effective using validated techniques of sensory, affective and behavioral aspects; scales for assessing pain and disability; encouraging attitudes; psychoeducation and strategies for stress relief and anxiety [17-18]. Moreover, it was observed success of cognitive behavioral interventions targeted approach for the treatment of patients with hypertension [19], heart disease [20], malignancy [21], skin diseases [22] and even surgery in pre and postoperatively [23].

The CBT shows such as a powerful ally for patients who have chronic, disabling and painful disease. In patients with lupus, another rheumatologic disease, that attacks the connective tissue, which is also systemic, chronic, painful and quickly degenerative, CBT showed positive results with reduction and control of pain and improved psychological functioning of these patients [24]. For fibromyalgia, another pain syndrome, CBT helped in extinguishing noxious behaviors of patients that suffer from this disease and behaviors that helped little as rest and excessive monitoring of bodily symptoms, and help manage the them with relaxation techniques and cognitive restructuring [25].

One of the differences of Cognitive Behavioral Therapy (CBT) is the work of relationship skills, management of lifestyle, social reintegration, control stress levels, cognitive restructuring, problem solving, and their contribution to to learn new skills to deal with difficulties [26]. For patients with chronic disease their contribution goes even further when the CBT proposes a model which covers the educational function of the disease, its symptoms, prognosis and medication [27].

The educational function becomes essential in the process of learning necessary for the patient completely understanding of disease and engages in treatment adherence. CBT has shown effective in the treatment and monitoring of numerous cases of clinical problems and drug treatment [28]. Studies on the application of cognitive behavioral model for the treatment of rheumatic diseases and, more specifically directed to the specifics of RA are still scarce in scientific literature, mainly when compared with the existing production evaluating the benefits of CBT for psychiatry disorders or even other medical conditions. [29-30].

Cognitive Behavioral Therapy for Rheumatoid Arthritis

As stated at the beginning of this chapter, RA is a chronic, debilitating and progressive disease. Day after day the patient will have increasingly limitation of their movements and watch each new deformation of a joint. Knowing that there will be not any cure or solution for each joint that has been affected. It is a painful syndrome and that means independent of temperature, time, or effort, the patient will feel pain; sometimes a small quantity of pain, others (especially during crises) almost insupportable. Patients even report that realize the affected region as if it is being "crushed" or "hammered". Medications will only control the progression of the disease, and that for the patient is a daily reminder of the pain that will follow the whole evolution of the disease each time the drug fails. For women, being affected by RA means sacrificing dreams like being a mother, or sacrificing his health permanently by opting the risk of pregnancy since she should stop taking all medications and consequently suffer the risk of reactivation the disease pictures with spikes of pain, inflammation and deformation of the joints until the end of pregnancy without the help of any emergency medication that could cause birth defects and other problems for the baby.

Beliefs of "magic cure" are common in these patients, which appears as unreal hopes of "waking up one day and having nothing more crooked and be healed", thoughts of worthlessness and being "a nuisance" are also frequent. they become increasingly dependent makes them develop increasingly a susceptible to depressive and suicide risk since they are patients who find themselves in a short period of time incapable of buttoning a dress and clothing alone [31], hold a fork and feed, turn the stove knob, open the registry, shower, open the door of the house, climbing stairs, combing his hair and brushing your teeth, take a shower and dry off, open a bottle or a can.

The work with patients with RA, as in any other health problem, starts with careful evaluation of the picture, and it involves since collect information from the complete history of the patient to psychological testing. A complete anamnesis and mental state examination are essential for two reasons: first this will be the first contact of the patient with the therapist, and it is from this moment the therapeutic bond, critical to proper functioning of the therapeutic setting will be created. Second, it is through anamnesis that arise diagnostic and therapeutic hypotheses as well as family and medical history of the patient, an important guide when it talks about any pathology, either clinical or psychological, as the CBT works with real hypothesis to structure the sessions [32].

Besides the initial interview, psychometric scales can be used in the clinical evaluation of these patients, which is quite useful for the detection and quantification of the severity of signs and psychopathological symptoms such as anxiety and depression, family and marital relationships variables, quality of life and even features especially relevant experience of RA patients such as pain, coping ability, level of disease activity, treatment adherence, among others.

Regarding the specific scales for rheumatic problems, some can be highlighted, as the Stanford Arthritis Center Health Assessment Questionnaire (HAQ), a scale used to classify the different levels of rheumatic diseases; the Medical Outcomes Study 36-Item Short-Form Health Survey (SF 36 and its reduced version of SF 12), to evaluate the perception of the disease by the patient; the Recent Onset Arthritis Disability (ROAD), which measures disease activity in RA patients with up to two years of illness.

There are even other specific scales for evaluation of patients with arthritis: Arthritis Impact Measurements Scales (AIMS), Functional Status Index (FSI); Arthritis Helplessness Index (AHI); Western Ontario and McMaster Universities Arthritis Index (WOMAC); among others. It is important to remember that due to joint compromise and often limb deformity, the patient may not have capacity to handle a pencil or other instruments that require fine motor skills, leading to the need of avoiding the choice of tests or other assessment tools that require the use of this resource.

Extra attention should be given to changes in scores suffered by the influence of organic responses in tests, for example, questions that ask if the patient "has been feeling tired lately" tend to generate positive responses or high scores due to symptoms of the disease and not necessarily because the patient fulfills the criterion of the construct which the instrument measures (eg.: depressive disorder). Therefore there is a need for a scale that discard physical symptoms only deepening in other areas such as the HADS (Hospital Anxiety and Depression Scale), which is a self-assessment scale developed to identify states of anxiety and depression in patients with clinical disease.

THE APPLICATION OF CBT FOR RHEUMATHOID ARTHRISTIS

The protocol for primary care patients with RA is divided into 12 sessions. In these sessions patients learn about their disease, treatment options, symptoms and progression of the clinical presentation, the chances of comorbidities, as well as learn to adjust their limitations. Pain management receives special attention in this Protocol, as it is the primary complaint in the lives of patients with arthritis. Throughout the process, dysfunctional beliefs are identified and modified. The patient will be instrumentalized, either by cognitive and behavioral techniques to deal with the difficulties of everyday life, seeking a more autonomous and independent mode of operation, but at the same time, enabling to identify potential support agents which the can count when they need help.

Since the evaluation was completed, the patients go for initial treatment sessions. It is important to consider that the evaluation phase also allowed the development of cognitive conceptualization of the case. The first session focuses on psychoeducation, wich can be defined as a flow of information between therapist and patient in order to listen and familiarize the patient about their problems and pathology, clarifying the implications and consequences of the established diagnosis [33]. It is a crucial step since one of the ways to prevent the opening of psychopathology pictures is the transmission of information about what can be expected from the evolution of the illness and along the treatment, avoiding the increasing of the anxiety before the unknown by the patient and also the formation of dysfunctional beliefs and the illness.

This step of psychoeducation is divided into contents strategically separated, in order that the patient can process calmly and clarify every doubt about the subject matter. Initially is provided information regarding AR as where the disease will be defined, the role of inflammatory markers, typical symptoms, prognosis, acute and remission phases, markers of pain, specific psychological symptoms and comorbidities. This first phase makes the patient automatically more adhered to treatment, because along with the transmission of information the patient perceives the opportunity to present issues and doubts that are never discussed with the medical team.

The main questions are presented by patients about how to deal with fears or prejudices caused by their situation. One example is the issue of morning stiffness, when the patient feels all his joints locked "as if they were plastered", a very common symptom for patients with RA and they usually interpret as "I did something wrong yesterday." In such cases, the patient can understand himself as "guilty" by the situation and move to avoid activities and tasks previously undertaken in the belief that could prevent the situation to recur. This practice, however, does not bring the expected benefit for the patient, that become even less active and, in most cases, more socially restricted, which can cause secondary damage. About the prejudice, note the difficulty of many patients as the "comments", "glances" and even avoidance behavior by the presence of the patient, manifested by others. Such situations are potentially generator of shame, sadness and frustration in many of these patients, in addition to causing great impact on their self-esteem. Therefore, they can choose again, by increasing insulation or respond with disproportionate reactions.

Simultaneously the information is provided to the patient, he is asked to constant provide feedback in order that the therapist can verify the proper understanding of the subject, avoiding the formation of new myths arising from possible misunderstanding. Moreover, the beliefs of patients are constantly evaluated according to the evolution of the topics presented in order to prevent the formation of dysfunctional beliefs, allowing immediately acting to eliminate them whenever identified.

In the next session, psychoeducation continues by addressing no longer the disease itself, but the whole pharmacological treatment. Empowered with accurate information about their pharmacotherapeutic possibilities involving its positive and negative aspects, the patient becomes more active in their treatment, which makes the compliance easier. At this stage, when needed, is used operative technique of decisional balance sheet for assistance concerning the use or not of "emergently" drugs (used during peaks and crises), better choice of treatment, side effects of each drug, the association between different drug classes, like it is the manner of implementation of each and effects of drug interactions.

An important note for this stage is the need for integration between the medical staff and the therapist for information about which drugs are being used, as well as dosages and previous attempts with other drugs. When applied decisional balance technique to the of sheet choices regarding the use of drugs, where the presence of the rheumatologist is recommended, to ensure any additional information that becomes necessary, ensuring total patient safety. In this second session the therapist can demystify some common beliefs of the patient as "RA made me gain weight" when in fact the patient is gaining weight by the continuous use of corticosteroids. Another benefit of this approach is that the patient becomes more collaborative to understand the therapy chosen by the doctor, avoiding posture of denial treatment.

Finally, psychoeducation is directed to the proper psychotherapy, where it will be explained to the patient as the cognitive model works and how it can benefit within the framework presented. Although some protocols begin to treat the patient with the clarification of the cognitive behavioral approach, in practice with patients diagnosed with RA is observed that the issue of disease is paramount and absolute center of attention and motivation of the patient, thereby clarifying the aspects relating to illness in the first place, allows the patient greater calm to focus on issues related to psychotherapeutic approach.

Still in the second session is made clarification on the importance of carrying out homework, which presents itself as an important practice, as much to justify the spacing between one session and another in the case of this research protocol, a week, as well as to accelerate results of the therapeutic process. Through the homework, the patient is also responsible, together with their therapist, for his treatment and has the opportunity to practice new skills learned beyond the therapeutic setting, continuing the progress made through the sessions and also extending to their environments of usual conviviality.

As the first home activity is proposed Registration of Daily Activities associated with the Pain Visual Analog Scale (VAS). The record of daily activities is a form that includes all days of the week and 24 hours a day, it works for monitoring some feeling or fact specific and previously agreed with the patient that occurs during everyday tasks, where each time the amendment or feeling occurs the patient must select the day and time that happened as a calendar of humor.

The use of VAS for pain assessment aims to assist patient in measuring his pain, with the objective of illustrating its evolution or the effectiveness of their treatment. It is divided into 10 points where each one has a meaning (0 would be the complete absence of pain and 10 the worst pain experienced by the patient) (34). Therefore the aim of the activity would be the monitoring of the pain (measured by VAS) throughout the day considering the patient's activities. For example: The patient woke up at 7 o'clock and was in pain considered for him as "4"; he should then go to the table and scoring woke up (on time 7 hours) and mark the score as "4". At 10 am while watching television, the patient had a change in his score for "6 points"; he must then pick the record and score within 10 hours regarding: watching TV and VAS 6 "" and so on. The next session (session 3), along with psychoeducation regarding the model of CBT will be a time for them to ask questions about the record and a new record is sent to the patient.

Time	Monday	Tuesday	Wednesday	Thursday	Friday	Saturday	Sunday
5-6	Sleeping	Sleeping	Sleeping	8 Woke up	Sleeping	Sleeping	Sleeping
6-7	Sleeping	3 Woke up	Sleeping	8 Took a SOS	5 Woke up	Sleeping	Sleeping
7-8	4 woke up	5 Took a Shower	Sleeping	Sleeping	5 Took a shower	Sleeping	Sleeping
8-9	Sleeping	6 got dressed	6 Woke up	Sleeping	5 Did my meal	Sleeping	Sleeping
9-10	6 Watching TV	3 Eat my breakfast	7 did a CBC	6 Woke up	6 Eat	Sleeping	Sleeping
10-11	6 Watching TV	6 Washed dishes	6 Eat my Breakfast	5 got out of bed	7 Washed dishes	3 Woke up	4 Woke up

Picture 1. Registration of daily activities table.

During the third session is made the introduction of scales designed to measure signs and symptoms of anxiety and depression and the level of disease evolution as a routine practice at the beginning of each meeting. At this point the scales are not used in order to diagnostic hypotheses, which has been previously conducted, but for monitoring therapeutic progress. By using valid and reliable instruments, guaranteed by means of objective measures of quality assured, adequate assessment of the benefits that the patient gets along the therapeutic process, avoiding erroneous attitudes caused by therapeutic decisions based on purely subjective perceptions regarding the improvement experienced by patient.

The patient is always informed about the purpose of each scale adopted and receives back the results attained by him. When needed (worsening or onset of new symptoms), the patient is referred for further consultation with the rheumatologist, because often patients with RA develop depression symptoms as collateral effect of medication, especially when he's using corticosteroids high doses for a long period of time . Anxiety conditions are also often associated with change of medication, worsening of symptoms, and increased expectations about the change of RA activity for active to inactive or asymptomatic. Furthermore, cognitive distortions are managed through Socratic questioning, downward arrow technique, questioning of labels and / or questioning assignments and meanings depending on the beliefs and distortions identified. This part aim the elimination of cognitive distortions and dysfunctional beliefs is constant throughout the therapeutic process.

The fourth session began by the review of homework, questioning the patient about what he was doing and thinking during recorded changes in VAS prioritizing the identification of activities linked to larger registries of pain. The patient is encouraged to make the association between activity and pain levels in order to identify those that provide the most comfortable moments and those with the greatest potential for severe pain. Generating tasks with frequency of stress and anxiety are associated with general worsening of symptoms of pain. This task allows the patient to better control his levels of pain along the day through smart choices, whenever possible, the activities carried out or even a balance between generating pain and others that do not cause these symptom activities, promoting a balance which may provide some relief to the patient. This method, like others, promotes the patient as an active being and returns him some capacity to control their symptoms.

From the correction of daily activities registration the patient becomes able to identify generating thoughts of stress that can be set to automatic thoughts involved in each situation, and we spent time working on them with the Socratic Method. The Socratic Method is made up of questions that the therapist should do for the patient with the goal of questioning the foundations of thoughts identified so. Since discovered that these fundamentals are absent, thoughts can be modified since then [35].

There is an association between the automatic thoughts of the patients of RA when analyzed and compared to VAS register. Usually what can be observed is that before performing a task he considers painful there is an increase in anxiety level, and from there the worsening of the picture of the patient. For example, the patient needs to water the plants with the hose. Automatically when he turns on the water he thinks "my pain will get worse," while he is performing this activity increases levels of muscle tension (caused by anticipatory anxiety and stress) and automatically there is a progressive increase in pain followed by thoughts "so I will not be good anymore", "I'm killing myself ","no use taking that amount of drugs, if I do not do my part", from there the patient has a crush on his mood, then he proceeds to try to reduce as much their day, which at the same time worsening the crisis, as with the avoidance of movement increases the stiffness and hence the pain, so riding his daily cycle.

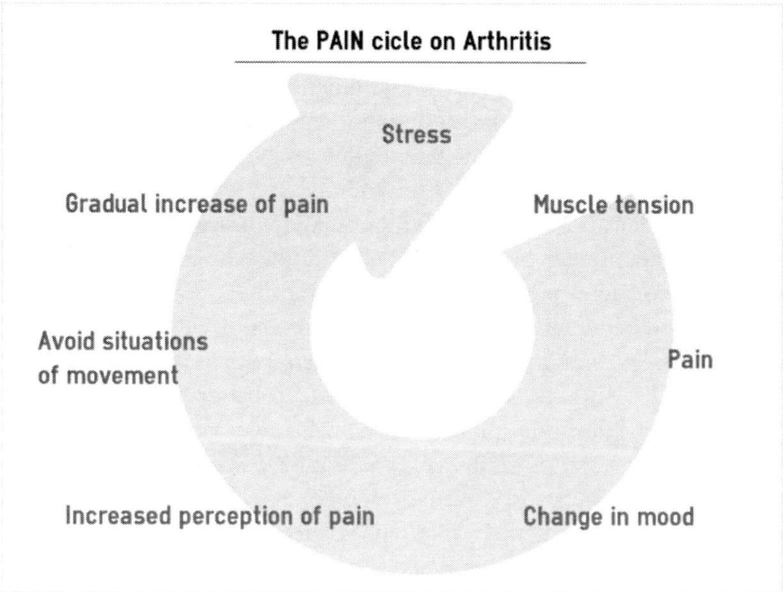

Picture 2. The pain circle on arthritis.

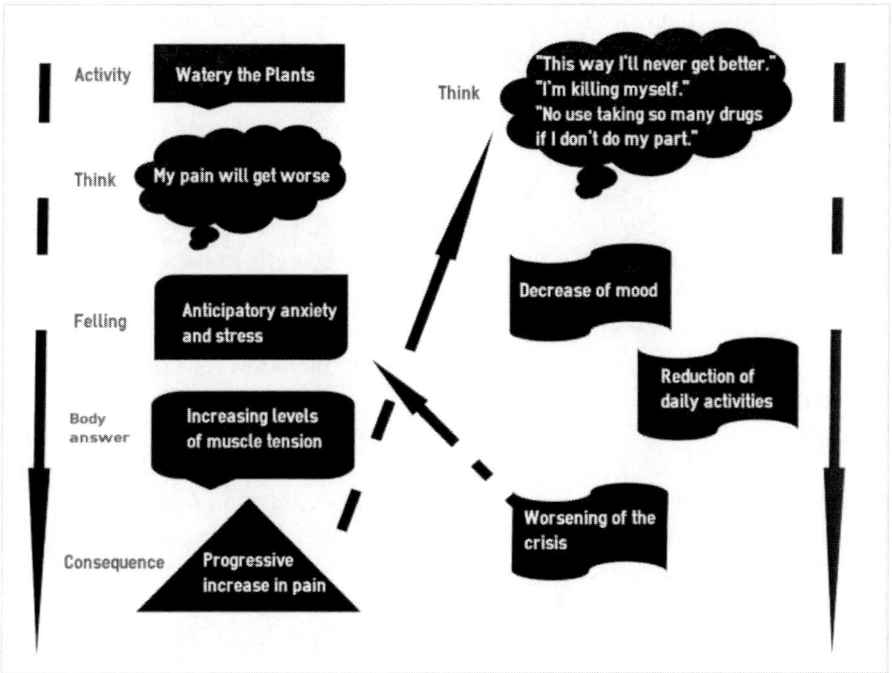

Picture 3. Problem-level formulation.

The fifth session starts with cognitive restructuring of dysfunctional thoughts identified in the previous session and over the previous week, and handle some central beliefs. A very common belief to the patient with RA is that they are causing their own illness and consequently there will be "a day when awake cured." This belief is a guiding for the patient in time to reduce activities in order to control his pain, to manage or modify their drug dosages with reduced symptoms and hardly has a good adhere to medical treatment. The belief in the magical healing can be associated with the fact most of the time patients were being treated for tendonitis to muscle strains before being diagnosed, but also in part to the denial that has an incurable disease and nothing you do can change its course.

In this session is also presented to the patient a control technique of anxiety that he can use in their daily life with the goal of breaking the cycle of pain: the deep breathing pressure. The choice of this method over others is by no need of respiratory control which would be very complicated to debilitated patients. It is then up to their achievement to inspire faster and stronger than the patient can, the patient being instructed to "put the maximum amount of air inside his body," then should hold their breath for as long as he can to release it slowly. The differential of this breathing technique is the time that the patient retains the air, it should contract the abdominal muscles and gently as if trying to channel the air out of a closed environment (air remains trapped) thus creating greater internal pressure.

The sixth session started with the aid of lists of signs and symptoms, differentiating between those that are related to anxiety and those characteristic of RA. The importance of this procedure is to help the patient to characterize anxiety so as to identify and control it before the start of the pain cycle. From this differentiation is initiated a training focus change [36] to control the anxiety, which consists on the enumeration and description of mental objects that are around this patient, but with a pre-established order for the patient with RA. For example: Show the patient that, on the left there are two fans, a red chair right over my head there are three combinations of phosphorescent lamps and beneath me a red carpet, this will change the focus from the stress situation. This technique originated from the technical focal distraction associated to the idea of muscle movement in the technique of Progressive Muscular Relaxing (PMR) [37], and progressed to this the need to involve a technique that makes the distraction and relieve the tensions cervical PMR without the stigma of contraction and relaxation which actually could be seen as an extremely limiting factor when presented to a public with serious malformations such as RA.

The seventh session a reevaluation must be done using the new implementation of all scales and comparing scores and an overall assessment of all the progress made from the beginning of treatment to the present moment. With this feedback the patient is encouraged to work through a timeline that considers facts milestones in their treatment from the beginning until then printed on it and its consequences.

The eighth session is different. Usually it coincides with the completion of clinical examinations and the routine visit to the rheumatologist. During this period there should also be the contact between therapist and medical team with the aim to know about the exams, if the patient will change the drug therapy, if the doctor noted change in the scoring box and anything you think pertinent to the case. Thus, the eighth session has its full focus on the evolution of medical and pharmacological therapy, including new decisions and adjustments to be made by the patient, being taken with the presence of cognitive behavioral therapist in rheumatologic consultation, both happening in integration.

At the ninth meeting it is begun to talk to the patient about techniques to solve problems associated with the disease. In this session we recall the joints most affected by RA (which has already been initially worked in psychoeducation), and ask the patient to enumerate the hierarchy with the difficulties and dependencies progression that the deterioration of each one of them can cause. From there we asked to establish quick and easy solutions to be implemented to ensure their integration and independence as much as possible in everyday life. Usually the patient here elaborates a bit more complex solutions than "a tool to open the bottle," he now considers living near any family, nursing homes or seeks to restructure their home to live downstairs.

In the tenth session after a fast feedback of the previous session we start by making a planning exercise. The objective of this exercise is to structure and plan alternatives for the life of the patient in 10 years considering disease progression topics such as reserve and finance expense, need for special care, the house or habits of life are approached but are also kept in focus strategies that enabling the patient to remain active and integrated into society in this session the patient often become very emotional when he thinks about how weak and dependent can he become in so little time.

In The eleventh session is done an overview of all the worked done so far. The patient is stimulated of remembering the topics of psychoeducation, each technique (making him play the breathing exercises and correcting any errors) and how to focusing on problem solving and planning. In the last session (twelfth), do an exercise to prevent relapse. In this exercise it is started to teach the patient to identify and evaluate the high-risk situations, mainly using VAS as a “thermometer”. This means, in practice, that patients with RA should know which situations that can promote those thoughts that lead, for example, the cycle of pain. As complementary to that financial strategies offer the possibility of keeping the patient self-monitoring by recording daily activities and prepare questionnaires for the assessment of risk situations. Patients should also be warned about the risks of relapse and fantasies and how much they can be harmful to the therapeutic progress. From then the patient is at discharge process only being received in maintenance sessions in spaces of time previously established for feedback and review of the current situation.

CASE REPORT

Stacy, a 35 years old female patient, was diagnosed with RA 18 months before the first meeting with the psychologist, and since then is in clinical pharmacological treatment with the classic combination of methotrexate and hydroxychloroquine, showing good response. She graduated in journalism and achieved master's and doctorate degree before the disease was identified, working in the area. She is married and has a 4 years old daughter. The rheumatologist appointed her to psychological evaluation when Stacy asks her what would happen if, hypothetically, she ingested 4 times the dosage of prescribed medications wondering if she would "die or just be sick for a while". The doctor then fills the routing questioning about the possibility of risk of suicide and depression.

In the first psychological session was performed a global assessment using, besides the anamnesis, scales as HADS, BSI, BHS, VAS and ROAD. Although the patient's illness seemed to be stagnant (ROAD), she had a severe depression (HADS = 20 also confirmed by the clinical interview), high rates of suicidal ideation (BSI = 25), hopelessness (BHS = 18) and VAS Mid pointing to pain only classified as "4", although the patient has said not taking any medicine for pain control that day (emergency drug).

After evaluation and the results obtained were presented to the patient enabling clarification on the overall situation. At that point it was also started the psychoeducation about the disease, when the patient said about her belief that she could still heal herself and reverse the small initial deformation that had the index finger of the right hand (the patient was right hand). She also talked about the 5 kg gained in the last month she believed was associated with medication. After giving the patient room to speak, the therapist explained the characteristics of the disease and how it worked. Dysfunctional beliefs about a full recovery were calmly corrected and the issue of weight gain clarified.

In the second session the VAS (3 points again without the use of any emergency drug) was performed. From a quick summary of the week in which the patient has narrated have had some peaks of pain, and again talk about weight gain (the patient complained have gained two extra kilos that week) was initiated psychoeducation about the medication in use, its consequences and how to manage that. All treatment options were explained as well as possible side effects of each one. The effects on the body and best time to use each drug were described. Stacy said she had used anti-inflammatory corticosteroids only for two months, while waiting to the results of the tests. Along the process she could identified other variables that could also collaborated for the weight gain like the recent replacement of the contraceptive pill, reduction on her habitual daily activity and the fact that she no longer does gym workout, swam or cardio exercises as she did before.

The next step in the session was the presentation of homework: The record of daily activities. It was explained that through it she could track situations that were generating peaks of pain throughout the week. It was agreed that when she woke up she would make the VAS, and that each change score write journaling what "I was doing / thinking / feeling".

In the third session the patient was again VAS scoring 4 points (without the use of any SOS drug), and the patient took the record for correction. Stacy said she struggled to write down everything that was asked and the VAS, claiming that when it came to what she was thinking, she had already forgotten. It was then agreed that the research would be reduced and that the VAS she was doing / thinking, discarding the feeling. Then was started the psychoeducation about the model of CBT and how the next sessions would be. Stacy, at the end, gave a positive feedback, saying she was feeling more confident now that her cure was in psychological treatment and also said she had understood why the doctor has chosen her medication over others.

Stacy was in the fourth session with VAS scoring 7 points and when she was asked, to say in her opinion, why that pain could have increased, she said she believed it was because she had quarreled with her husband. The patient reported having identified throughout the week that higher levels of stress also increased the pain. Each situation that Stacy developed peak pain or increase in their VAS score in more than two points in the week was then analyzed.

The patient placed in ascending order of worst situations: fight with her daughter (which claimed to do fairly often lately because of difficult eating habits of the child), take the dog for a walk (the other patient claimed that Pitt Bull gave great pulls on her arm too worsening her pain), quarrel with her husband (the patient assumed to be impatient with him) and last consultation with a rheumatologist (which she pointed out as being the most stressful and difficult of all situations). The patient was then taught how to recognize each sign of increased anxiety and a breathing exercise was taught to control stress.

In this exercise, the goal of the patient was inflate their lungs as quickly as possible and with the greatest amount of air that believe fit. Then Stacy should hold her breath and force a contraction of the abdominal muscles, as if restricting all air from inside the body for a unique way: to her head, as if dropping the nose, but without letting it escape. Then the patient would leave all the air out of her mouth in a controlled manner, leaving as little as possible to escape, and was told that she could feel a slight dizziness but it was normal, and then feel her heart beat much more slowly than before.

The exercise was trained for three consecutive times, until the patient could perform the maneuver alone and completely, reaching the stated goal. It was agreed that despite the most anxiogenic situations was identified, Stacy should continue performing the activity log. Stacy came to the fifth session with 10 minutes late, limping and complaining of much pain in her left knee, her VAS was 5 points despite that, and the patient was questioned about when the pain started. She said she had gone to the doctor and he said that there was not any sign of inflammation and modification of disease activity when compared to the previous query. Stacy said she was overjoyed and asked when she could stop taking the medication, and then the doctor said that if she stopped taking the disease would return to attack her.

Stacy then said she believes have not yet healed by the small amount of sunbathing she had taken since been ill, and she was sure that if the sunbathing duration was increased for at least one hour per day in a month of exposure she would not have RA anymore. This belief is incorrect and can generate unreachable expectations. The patient was questioned about the basic characteristics of RA, and responded promptly to be a progressive, degenerative and chronic disease, showing having intellectual knowledge of all previously transmitted.

The patient was asked which other chronic illness she knew and she reported that her father had a chronic heart disease. Then she was asked at what time of life her father had been cured of the disease, the patient then automatically understand the concept of chronic, but cannot reproduce her speech externally. Then it was introduced the restructuring model of dysfunctional thoughts in order to change this cycle.

Stacy was in the sixth session with VAS 3 points; she was more collaborative and lively. The patient was asked to make two different lists in order to separate the symptoms related to RA and those related to anxiety, which was attended with some difficulty, since she initially tried scoring the trembling in the body as a symptom of arthritis. Readily passed to the first session leaflet describing all symptoms related to the disease, and since then the patient has achieved the goal of the exercise.

RA Symptoms	Anxiety Symptoms
* Pain	* Chest pressure
* Fatigue	* Palpitations
* Stiffness	* Cold sweats
* Lack of movement	* Chills
* Swelling, fever	* Butterflies in the stomach
* Lack of appetite	* Trembling in the body
* Difficulty to open things	* Breathlessness
* Pain to sit	* Blurred vision

Picture 4. Table of symptoms.

As Feedback she reported be feeling a little more resigned to the disease, better understanding her picture and her symptoms and she is controlling her peaks of pain independently, but reported having difficulty to do the respiratory training in situations that involved her visits the doctor. It was taught as an exercise as alternative option of association between focal distraction and systematic, where the goal of the patient would be mentally enumerate objects that were around her respecting a pre-established order. Stacy should then look to your left side and count objects of the same type (3 points blue chairs), then look to the right side and do the same with other objects (1 aluminum trash can), then doing the same with objects above it and below (2 ceiling fans / 2 green carpets).

At the seventh session was held the initial battery of scales again. Stacy was with VAS 4 points, HADS 12 points, zeroed BSI, BHS 7 points and extremely more motivated. Stacy was then asked to create a timeline and which she narrated from her peak moments of treatment until that moment and the consequences arising out of it.

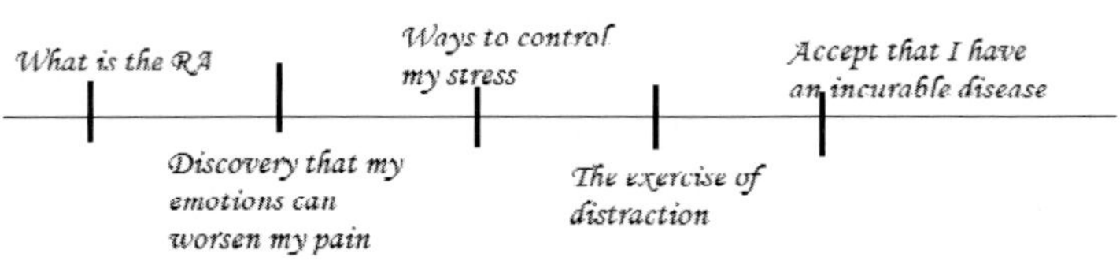

Picture 5. Timeline of the treatment by the point of the patient.

Stacy then says that the result of all the milestones of the treatment was make her able to make decisions not by emotions but now that rationally understand her illness, how to treat it and how to remove many of its symptoms. Stacy pointed out that the most difficult milestone was faced the fact that she had an incurable disease, but from then realized that she could still fight for her health.

At the eighth session, Stacy had an appointment with her doctor to evaluate her medical exams. In this consultation (with the presence of the therapist) the patient was informed that she would not need to change her medication and that her illness was responding well to drug therapy. The doctor also praised the progress in therapy, and scheduled the following query already leaving with new applications for examination. At the ninth session the focus was in solving problems related to the disease. A doll with the figure of a person was given to Stacy, that was asked to identify which joints are most affected in RA.

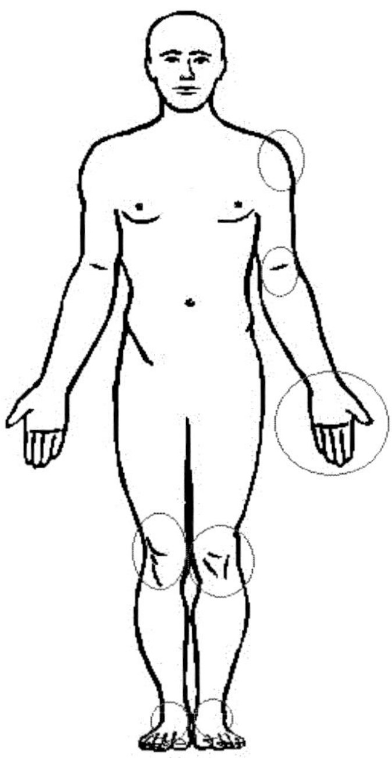

Picture 6. Most affected joints pointed by the patient.

Stacy runs the requested task without any difficulty, circling shoulder, elbow, wrist and hand, knees and ankles. Then she was asked to think about each difficulty she would have in case the disease progresses in each of the joints. The patient lists that the disease progressing shoulder becomes difficult to lift her arms to wash and comb her hair. If the joint were the elbow, the biggest challenge would probably endure carrying things like dishes or even the clothes pressed, but readily established as a solution using a cart to support the activities. Then the patient enumerated that if the inflammation in her hand and wrist evolve, could not feed herself, write, open and close things, come home and support when needed down the stairs, she pointed to this problem that could hire a diarist or an accompanying person as her health plan allow this type of care. Then when evaluating restricted to the evolution of inflammation of the knees activities, Stacy reported to have already given it much thought, could no longer live where she was, since her house was a duplex and to enter in her apartment should climb two flights of stairs, therefore would move to the house of her sister that was flat or if there was any impediment, would live in a care home. And when asked about the feet, the patient said she could no longer walk or even stay with shoes depending on the level of deterioration, but as in the previous answer, could move and acquire a wheelchair to get around. Each situation was analyzed in detail considering possible prejudices and attitudes that the patient could take in the future to deal with the problems as well as skills to identify possible resources, both financial and regarding the identification of persons that would support the face of new challenges arising from their disease, were trained.

In the tenth session Stacy was asked to write a list of things she would do in 10 years taking into account her disease. The patient begins to cry and says she is reviewing its plans, as one of the most important was spending a month in India, and she knows she cannot do that. When asked the reason she reports that the lack of hygiene, difficulty in finding good hospitals and the evolution of her illness until then would be limiting, and would depend on which medication she was taking at the time. Stacy was then stimulated to do a real budget of each alternative given in the previous session and more the realization of a dream. She elaborates planning starting from sickness assistance, and some additional income that she already own, putting about 60% of this income to issues related disease such as mobility, service, staff and medicines, and reports that will have to change her dreams and had begun to search places adapted for wheelchair users what "would be the worst picture of my illness in 10 years."

The eleventh session Stacy is encouraged to make a review of what was then worked up, and actively plays from psychoeducation to relaxation exercises taught. She shows herself participative, make small questions about the drug therapy and respiratory exercise. She is reevaluated and scores point to an absence of depression and suicidal ideation. At the twelfth session work is all focused on the prevention of relapse and the patient showed massive control in dealing with her pain and reduce the peaks considerably increasing the time between one crisis and another. The patient should then be discharged only to the first maintenance sessions once a month.

Conclusion

RA is a chronic, progressive, debilitating, inflammatory disease of autoimmune origin, which affects the joints of the patient. Its symptoms include fever, weakness and loss of appetite; it also causes the patient beyond the progressive deformities, chronic pain, stiffness followed by loss of movement and function of the affected area, excessive wear of each articular disc, tendon injuries and the reduction and poor quality of life of the patient.

It is considered a priority the development of protocols and creating new techniques to minimize the effects and symptoms of clinical diseases that even on medication influence can alter the individual daily activities. Cognitive behavioral therapy has tools to help facilitate this whole procedure in adherence to treatment, minimizing the pain, teaching patient to overcome and adapt to illness, working his expectations and giving another meaning to his life without being dependent on the disease; for this there are ongoing research within this field, aimed to encompass the maximum possible pathologies and symptoms. Nevertheless the field of rheumatic diseases is still poorly studied, creating a gap between the practices used when comparing the other diseases like cancer and HIV.

This protocol shows a form of intervention in the presented RA population, which has proven very effective in many points. It facilitates understanding of key aspects of the disease as characteristics, symptomatology, choice of pharmacological therapy and prognosis, helping the patient to ask questions and giving the confidence he needs to be more active during their clinical treatment. The Protocol also requires a change in ways of engaging the patient to help understanding of the mechanisms of pain and its control. The protocol also works with the expectations of the patient and thoughts that can modify and even worsen the symptoms of RA, teaching him how to identify and fight them. Finally the protocol maintains the issues related to planning and problem solving in which the patient comes to see situations which may pass in accordance with the evolution of the disease and its worsening symptoms.

This protocol aims to be a facilitator in the intervention to the patient with RA. More studies, nevertheless, are needed with a larger population and addressing different biases in medical treatment. Moreover, patients receiving different types of medical treatment or who have comorbidities with other non-psychiatric conditions, as well as in different stages of the disease should have these aspects considered for adaptation of the basic protocol.

REFERENCES

[1] Alexopulos GS, Buckwalter K, Olin J, Martinez R, Waitscott C, Krishann KRR. Comorbidity of late life depression: an opportunity for research on mechanisms and treatment. *Biol Psychiatry.* 52, 2002, pp. 543-58.

[2] Hymovich, D.p. and Hagopian, G.a. *Chronic Illness in Children and Adults: a Psychosocial Approach.* Philadelphia : W.B. Sauders, 1992.

[3] Aceves – Avila F. J., Medina F., Fraga A. The antiquity of rheumatoid arthritis : a reappraisal. *J Rheumatol.* 2001, 28, pp. 751-57.

[4] Fellet, Aloysio J, Tavares, Agostinho and Scotton, Antônio Scafuto. Rheumatoid arthritis. *Revista Brasileira de Medicina.* 58, 2001, pp. 102-11.

[5] Walsh NC, Crotti TN, Goldring SR. Rheumatic diseases: the effects of inflammations on boné. *Immunol.* 208, 2005, pp. 228-51.

[6] Young A, Koduri G. Extra-articular manifestations and complications oh rheumatoid arthritis. *Best Pract Res Clin Rheumatol.* 21, 2007, pp. 907-27.

[7] Goodson NJ, Farragher TM, Symmons DP. Rheumatoid factor, smoking, and disease severity: associations with mortality in rheumatoid arthritis. *J Rheumatol.* 35, 2008, pp. 945-9.

[8] Laurindo IMM, Ximenes AC, Lima FAC, Pinheiro GRC. *Projeto Diretrizes: Artrite Reumatóide, Diagnóstico e Tratamento.* s.l. : Sociedade Brasileira de Reumatologia, 2002.

[9] Fishbain DA, Cutler R, Rosomoff HL, Rosomoff RS. Chronic Pain-Associated Depression: Antecedent or Consequence of Chronic Pain: A review. *Clin J Pain.* 13, 1997, pp. 116-37.

[10] Schieir O, Thombs BD, Hudson M, Taillefer S, Steele R, Berkson L, Bertrand C, Couture F, Fitzcharles MA, Gagné M, Garfield B, Gutkowski A, Kang H, Kapusta M, Ligier S, Mathieu JP, Ménard H, Mercille S, Starr M, Stein M, Zummer M, Baron M. Symptoms of Depression Predict the Trajectory of Pain Among Patients with Early Inflammatory Arthritis: A Path Analysis Approach to Assessing Change. *J Rheumatol.* 36, 2009, pp. 231-39.

[11] Duarte MB, Rego MAV. Depression and clinical illness: comorbidity in a geriatric outpatient clinic. *Cad. Saúde Pública.* 23, 2007, pp. 691-700.

[12] Blair, t. and Ramones, V.a. Education as Psychiatric Intervention: The Cognitive-Behavioral Context. *J Psychosoc Nurs.* 35, 1997, Vol. 12, pp. 29-36.

[13] Blair, T. Integration and Synthesis: Cognitive Behavioral Therapies Within the Biological Paradigm. *J Psychosoc Nurs.* 34, 1996, Vol. 12, pp. 26-31.

[14] Odegard S, Finset A, Mowinckel P. Pain and psychological health status over a 10- year period in patients with recent onset rheumatoid arthritis. *Ann Rheum Dis.* 66, 2007, pp. 1195- 1201.

[15] Dissanayake RK, Bertouch JV. .Psychosocial interventions as adjunct therapy for patients with rheumatoid arthritis: a systematic review. *Int J Rheum Dis.* 13, 2010, Vol. 4, pp. 324-34.

[16] Cuijpers P, Van Straten A. Internet-administered cognitive behavior therapy for health problems: a systematic review. *Journal of Behavioral Medicine.* 31, 2008, pp. 169-177.

[17] Beck, J. S. Cognitive therapy: Basics and beyond. New York: Guilford.

[18] Lam DH, McCrone P, Wright K, Kerr N. Cost effectiveness of relapse prevention cognitive therapy for bipolar disorder: 30-month study. *Br J Psychiatry.* 186, 2005, pp. 500-6.

[19] Butler AC, Chapman JE, Foreman EM, Beck AT. The empirical status of cognitive-behavioral therapy: a review of meta-analyses. *Clin Psychol Rev.* 26, 2006, Vol. 1, pp. 17-31.

[20] AT., Beck. The current state of cognitive therapy: a 40 year retrospective. *Arch Gen Psychiatry.* 62, 2005, Vol. 9, pp. 953-9.

[21] AC, Neves Neto. Cognitive-behavioral therapy and irritable bowel syndrome. *Rev. Psiq. Clín.* 28, 2001, Vol. 6, pp. 350-355.

[22] B., Castro. Contributions of cognitive-behavioral therapy in palliative care. *Revista Psicologia, Diversidade e Saúde.* 1, 2012, Vol. 1, pp. 101-8.

[23] Thorn, Beverly E. *Cognitive Therapy for Chronic Pain: A Step-by-Step Guide. New Yor:* Wiley, 2001.

[24] Greco, C. M., Rudy, T. E., Manzi, S. Effects of a stress-reduction program on psychological function, pain, and physical function of systemic lupus erythematosus: a randomized controlled trial. *Arthritis & Rheumatism.* 51, 2004, pp. 625-34.

[25] Goldenberg D, Kaplan K, Nadeau M. A prospective study of stress reduction, relaxation response therapy. *Scandinavian Journal Rheumatology,.* s94, 1992, p. 47.

[26] Wright JH, Beck AT, Thase ME. *Cognitive therapy, in Textbook of Clinical Psychiatry, 4th ed.* Washington, DC : American Psychiatric Publishing, 2003.

[27] Callaham, M.A. & Bauer, M.S. Psychosocial Interventions for Bipolar Disorder. *The Psychiatric Clinics of North América.* 22, 1999, pp. 675-88.

[28] Satterfield, Jason M. A cognitive-behavioral approach to the beginning of the end of life minding the body : facilitator guide. *New York : Oxford University Press, 2008.*

[29] White, Craig A. *Cognitive Behaviour Therapy for Chronic Medical Problems: A Guide to Assessment and Treatment in Practice. New York, John Wiley & Sons Ltd, 2001.*

[30] Marques Neto JF, Gonçalves ET, Barros EFO. Multicentric study of the prevalence of adult rheumatoid arthritis in Brazilian population samples. *Rev Bras Reumatol.* 33, 1993, Vol. 5, pp. 169-73.

[31] Cade, NV. Group therapy for patients with arterial hypertension. *Rev. Psiq. Clín.* 28, 2001, Vol. 6, pp. 300-4.

[32] Luz, JAG and Pergher, GK. CBT in preoperative and postoperative cardiovascular surgery. *Brazilian Journal of Cognitive Therapies.* 6, 2010, Vol. 1, pp. 173-194.

[33] Moorey S; Greer S. Oxford Guide to CBT for People with Cancer (Oxford Guides to Cognitive Behavioural Therapy). *New York: Oxford University Press 2012.*

[34] Motta, AKF, et al. Bariatric Surgery Program: Therapeutic Group Post Surgical As Instrument Of Interdisciplinary Intervention. *revista hugv.* 10, 2011, Vol. 2, pp. 31-4.

[35] Chida Y, Steptoe A , Hirakawa N , Sudo N , Kubo C. The effects of psychological intervention on atopic dermatitis: a systematic review and meta-analysis. *International archives of allergy and immunology.* 144, 2007, Vol. 1, pp. 1-9.

[36] Matos, GN, et al. Discourses of patients with rheumatoid arthritis regarding their social relationships: a study from the psychological perspective. *Sau. & Transf. Soc.* 1, 2010, Vol. 1, pp. 99-105.

[37] Jacobson, E. *Progressive relaxation.* Chicago : University of Chicago Press, 1983.

[38] Leahy, Robert L.. *Cognitive Therapy Techniques: A Practitioner's Guide. New York: Guilford Press,* 2003.

[39] Ribeiro, NPO, et al. Anxiety, depression and suicidal ideation in patients with rheumatoid arthritis in use of methotrexate, hydroxychloroquine, leflunomide and biological drugs. *Compr Psychiatry.* 54, Nov 2013, Vol. 8, pp. 1185-9.

About the Authors

Adriana Cardoso Silva, Ph. D.

Professor of Institute of Psychiatry – Federal University of Rio de Janeiro (IPUB/ UFRJ); Professor of the Post-Graduated Program of Psychiatry and Mental Health – IPUB/ UFRJ. Researcher at National Institute of Science and Technology for Translational Medicine (INCT-TM/ CNPq).

Alexandre Rafael de Mello Schier

Psychology; Doctorate degree student of the Post-Graduated Program of Psychiatry and Mental Health - Institute of Psychiatry – Federal University of Rio de Janeiro (IPUB/ UFRJ)

Natalia Pinho de Oliveira Ribeiro

Psychology; Doctorate degree student of the Post-Graduated Program of Psychiatry and Mental Health - Institute of Psychiatry – Federal University of Rio de Janeiro (IPUB/ UFRJ)

INDEX

#

A

B

C

D

I

J

K

L

M

N

O

P

Q

R

S

T

U

V

W

Y

Z